MAKING A LIFE

MAKING A LIFE

— • —

Career, Commitment, and the Life-Process

— • —

GENE RUYLE

The Seabury Press • New York

1983
The Seabury Press
815 Second Avenue
New York, N.Y. 10017

Printed in the United States of America

Library of Congress Cataloging in Publication Data

Library of Congress Cataloging in Publication Data

Ruyle, Gene, 1935–
    Making a life.

    Bibliography: p.
    1. Adulthood.   2. Occupations.   3. Life.   4. Conduct
of life.   I. Title.
HQ799.95.R88   1983   158'.1   83-8953
ISBN 0-8164-2408-X

To the life of:

Everett, my father,
   who gave me theatre, wanderlust, and life;

Naomi, my mother,
   who gave me poetry, religion, and life;

Richard R. Baker III, my padre,
   who used philosophy and theology to open
      me to the immensity of life;

Sidney Jourard, my teacher and friend,
   who pointed me in the direction of life;

Vinnie O'Connell, Sam Keen, and Tom Hanna, my comrades,
   who challenged me to find my path to it;

Joy, my wife and staunch mate,
   who travels with me on her own way, sharing
      all of the ups and downs, and knows my
         soul as does no other;

. . . and to Gina, Mark, Kelly, Paul, and Ivan, my children,
   who each mark my life with a special something that I
      would never want it to be without;

and with grateful acknowledgment to: Jessie Woodward; Frs. Donald F. Haviland and Joseph P. Hollifield; Hazel Williams, speech teacher; Pvts. James L. McElroy and John P. Furleigh, USMC; Cpls. John D. Burke and Carroll C. Barrows, and Col. R. F. Klein, MACS-5, MACG-1, 2nd Marine Air Wing, USMCALF, Edenton, NC; Professor James A. Pait and Dr. Leland L. Zimmerman; Spook Shonbrun, theatre director; the Very Rev. Fred G. Yerkes; Clifford L. Stanley, theologian, and A. T. Mollegen, apologist; Holt H. Graham, mentor; Charles P. Price of Virginia Theological Seminary; the Revs. Earle Cornelius Page and William Washburn Lillycrop; Maj. Roy Woods, RCAF (Ret.); the Revs. Paul Ritch, Lex Mathews, and Robert Oliver; Jerome I. Berlin, PhD, and Bob Donnelly, truly a priest — and Kathy Isenberg, Phil Arnold, Dick Noakes, and Steve Friedlander of the

Human Development Institute; Caroline and Bill Friesner, Jack and Jane Pollack, Peggy Tyndale, Preston and Marian Stevens, and the Revs. Robert H. Johnson and John J. Porter of Holy Innocents, Atlanta; Nell Bennett and Grandma Crider; Mary Kahaian and Lance; the Very Rev. Urban T. Holmes, Lueta Bailey, Carol Jean Kennedy, Pamela Sanford, Ed Hartley, and the Revs. Tom Bowers and Charlie Sumners of Kanuga days gone by; Nancy Drew and Mary Crowley, and Reid Isaac and Bob Gilday; Jane Linville; Roy P. Fairfield, innovative educator, and Charles Martin, PhD, of Union Graduate School; the Rt. Rev. Hamilton West, and the Rt. Revs. Frank Cerveny and Bennett Sims; Billie Burnham; Jim Coyle and Ace Hagebak of the Southern Institute for Human Resources, and Bonnie Davis and Travis Holtzclaw of the U.S. Depts. of Labor and HEW; Henrietta and Joe Priest of workshops in Ocala; Robbie Richter, Joe Few, and Elaine Turcotte of Caulderwood Management (for their natural kindness, as well as the space, copier, and typewriter where the manuscript was typed); Eugenia Abernathy; the Rev. Lavan B. Davis of the Florida panhandle, the Rev. Robert W. Myers and Evelyn, the Rev. Robert A. Boone, and Sarah Hayes, of St. Christopher's, Pensacola; the Very Rev. John E. Banks, and the Newberry Conference of the Diocese of Upper South Carolina; Hans Hoelzer; the Rev. Dan P. Matthews and the staff and good people of St. Luke's, Atlanta; Maria and John Hollingsworth, and Ralph Scott of a well-kept McDonalds; Cindy, Helga, and Kim (who repeatedly burned their hands at Dunkin' Donut when pouring the coffee into my thermos that kept endless days and nights of typing going); Tamara Bazzle; George Kaysian, Elise Stokes, and Edra Riley (the "weeping willows"), and Mary Zinsser and the whole group at Canterbury Court — and to others too numerous to name but not to remember. Each one of them has given something that helped me personally in bringing out a book which was, with no exaggeration, a lifetime in the making;

. . . and, finally, to all of those still laboring to keep their dreams alive and to make them fully real.

CONTENTS

1 • JUST BETWEEN US 1

Putting This Book in Its Place 1

What It Is About and What It Is For 2

Making Something of It 4

2 • TO BE SOMEBODY 6

What You Have, What You Are, What You Do 6

To Know Life 10

Look Before You Leap 11

Experience the Thing Itself 13

The Life That Is Yet to Come 22

3 • IN A TIME LIKE THIS   24

You Weren't Born Yesterday   24

Who, What, When, Where, How, and Why   26

Things Aren't What They Used to Be   27

What Is Happening in Our Time?   29

What It Means   31

Why It Is So Hard to See   32

From Now On   33

4 • MAKING A LIFE   36

Look at What You've Done   36

The Sign of Life — *reading the signs*   37

The Sense of Life — *coming to terms*   37

The Stuff of Life — *molding the clay*   39

The Sign, Sense, and Stuff of Life — *experiencing it all* 44

A Matter of Words   48

5 • IN THE RAGGED RAW REAL   50

A Self and a Story   50

Life Has Its Moments   51

Going Through the Motions   52

Who Do You Think You Are?   59

A View from the Stern   62

6 · SEEING THE SOUL   64

Why Bring That Up?   64

For All to See   66

Coming into View   67

Modes of Human Becoming   68

The Dis-eases and Diseases of the Soul   120

What Your Being is Becoming   121

7 · SENSING THE SPIRIT   126

At Any Moment   126

A Matter of Life and Death   127

What to Look For   177

Spirituality, Sexuality, and That Which Stirs   130

8 · MOVING ON TO MORE   133

Nothing Quite Like Experience   133

You Know You Have It in You   134

Time for Moving on to More   135

Glossary   136

Locator   140

For Those Who Want to Read More   151

MAKING A LIFE

·1·

JUST BETWEEN US

PUTTING THIS BOOK IN ITS PLACE

A book is just ink, paper, and dried glue until someone comes along, picks it up, opens it, and starts to read. Then an amazing thing happens which even today we are not able to explain or fully understand. For as the eye moves along to take in what it sees, what are nothing more than marks on a page are transformed wondrously into *words*. Each word starts to stir like a little Pinocchio that can act on its own to speak, shout, soothe, sing, sting or startle. Now the book, a lifeless lump before, can "say something." When it does, the door to a whole new realm is opened, and in that moment we enter into the world of what things mean.

All of this happens in an instant. It is part of something greater which we are doing all of the time. We *make sense* out of life each and every minute, and we live in the sense that we make. But we rarely notice this or pay it any attention. For instance, you are doing this now as you read this very sentence; yet do you notice it, or would you if your attention had not been called to it? Probably not. Most likely you would have gone on the way the rest of us do, focusing on whatever was before you at the moment (or on what you happened to "feel" or "have on your mind"), and on what you took it to mean, aware only of the end product —

taking this as something simply *there* rather than as something you yourself brought into being.

So . . . in reading these first few lines, and in noticing what you have done, you have just managed to bring to the surface the fact of your own participation in one of the most important human acts of all. (The only other acts that can rival it are birth and death, our coming into and passing out of existence; yet this act alone connects these two with all that happens in between.) Why is making sense so important? Well, since your life is real, what you do with it also becomes real. The sense you have made of these opening lines has now become a part of what has truly happened. In doing this you have already made, regardless of how brief or tiny it is, a piece of reality for all eternity.

WHAT IT IS ABOUT AND WHAT IT IS FOR

What this book is about, therefore, is not in these pages. It is in you. The book is about what you are doing with your life, what you are making out of what you are. It is about "doing your stuff," as we say when we have in mind persons who are finding and using that which is really theirs to do.

Thus, you are the book's main character, its central figure, the one around whom everything in it revolves. "But," you may say, "you don't even know me." True, and you do not know me either. Still, that does not keep either of us from sensing and being aware of that basic aliveness, so uniquely stamped in each of us, which is going on in us both right now (as it is in every other human being on earth too). We do not need to know each other, though, to know what it is and that it is there.

Our lives come in a diversity of sizes, shapes, shades, and situations. For example, you may just now be getting ready to choose a career and make that all-important decision about what you primarily intend to do with your life. On the other hand, you may be in the middle of the increasingly common change of moving from one career to another. Or perhaps neither is the case, because you have had a satisfying career for several years and plan to continue to ride it right on up to retirement. Regardless of what your present situation may be though, or mine, as we get up in the morning and as we sleep through the night, from our very first breath to our very last, we humans are all involved in the same thing. We take hold of the stuff of life, and then we each in our own way *mold and shape it into what we are.* That is what this book is about, making a life.

But what is it for? Perhaps you know exactly what you most want to do with your life. Or, maybe you do not yet have the slightest idea. What have you mainly given your life to so far? To preparation and getting ready? If so, for what? Or instead, has it been given to accomplishing and achieving? If that is so, how is it going? To whom do you or have you given much of yourself? To several people, a few, none at all? What is the path you are taking at present or the direction you are moving in? Is it the one you want to follow in the future?

Those who honestly know and care about you, and these seldom make more than a handful, can probably give you some genuine help with these questions. Outside this small social sphere, advice is offered, free and not so free, by the "expert" and the "experienced." The shortcoming in this is not that these people do not know what they are talking about (many of them know a great deal, though there is always an abundant supply of the other kind), but rather that they know so little about who they are talking to. Advice is mostly offered by people who do not know us all that well, and whom we do not know well enough to see if they even follow it themselves. The surest way to find lasting and worthwhile answers to such questions is to make use of what you have learned by now of who you are and who you are not.

This all brings us right back to where we started — with

you. The working premise that will run throughout this book and upon which this whole venture is based is that *you know more about your life than anyone else does and are thus the one to decide what to do with it and where to go from here.* (If this premise strikes you as too self-centered and you would prefer something more objective, you might try noticing how much of what passes for "objectivity" is really only someone else's subjectivity.) But therein lies the rub! Because most of us find it exceedingly difficult to get at this knowledge, to lift it up and bring it out, so it can be used to make our way further. This is a book to help you do that. It is a tool, nothing more; not an end in itself, but something to be used for something else. Like any tool, it is a thing to do something with. Now that you know what the book is about as well as what it is for, we have put it in its place; and you can plainly see why it is something that is, truly, just between us.

MAKING SOMETHING OF IT

If it turns out that this book helps you catch a glimpse here and there of your own special quality of life, which is as unique as your fingerprint, then the credit will be yours and so will be the discovery. However, if anything in these pages should go against what you have learned from life, do not hesitate to leave these words behind. Let us part company at that point as you heed the more important voice of your own experience.

Remember to remain true to that movement of life which you sense is your own, and let nothing undercut your trust in your own ability to read it. For this is your birthright as a human being. Apart from it there is no way for anyone to ever know what his or her life is or what it means. Without it, one is lost. It is not anything that can be taken from you, but it can be let go of and given away. If that has ever happened to you, you know it; or if it ever does, something in you will know. Then you must move to reclaim and regain it, which can be done by risking again to choose and use that which brings you life. For this is the reach through which life reaches us once more, enabling us to get on with that which is certainly our grandest task: *making a life.*

A human life does not just happen, nor does it unfold automatically. It is made. From beginning to end we make sense of every moment lived, which we experience as impulses, notions, urges, thoughts, feelings, and hunches of every kind. Whether these be vague and fleeting or move clearly into words and deeds, it is just such sensings as these that, when added all together, come to make up the life lived by someone like you or me.

Making Sense

The sense
man makes
in turn
makes man.
To turn
to what
one can't
understand,
is better
than to
turn it
into what
one can.

·2·

TO BE SOMEBODY

"I" you say, and are proud of the word. But greater is that in which you do not wish to have faith — your body and its great reason, that does not say "I," but does "I."

—*Nietzsche*

Life is the word that describes us most. No other word can thread through what we have, do, and are, together. Without the three of these our understanding of human beings becomes unraveled and falls apart.

Because life is this big, and is constantly churning and changing, it is hard for us to know. We miss so much of what life is, but the tragedy is that we miss it without ever knowing that we missed it. This tragedy befalls us unseen and unheard, but it is no less disastrous or fatal. The only way any of us can avoid this common catastrophe is to deal with life directly as we try to bring the self to the surface by entering as fully as we are able into what our life actually is and who we really are.

WHAT YOU HAVE, WHAT YOU ARE, AND WHAT YOU DO

Some people say they know far more about their lives than they care to, while others lament not yet having found out who they are. But the greatest number pay very little at-

6

tention to such matters at all, so engrossed are they in the occupations and preoccupations of each day. Hence, "the majority," about which so much is said, is not actually silent nor ever very still. Let us look a little more clearly, then, at what it means to live as a human being.

What You Have Is Unique: You Are Aware

We speak of "having things" — not only external possessions, but urges, ideas, memories, dreams, desires, sensations, and experiences of every kind. And we speak of having still other things that cannot be seen, such as aims, goals, ideals; and we even speak of "having life."

We *have* life through our awareness of it. Without *having*, we humans would amount to only *being* and *doing* — and any working machine is capable of that, be it an idling engine or a functioning computer. The life you have, your awareness, is unique. Even if you were cloned, the awareness you had would still be your own possession (just as the clone would have his or hers too). It is yours alone and can belong to no other.

Awareness always has an object. You are always aware *of* something. Only in awareness is there the necessary distance, the room it takes, for the *otherness* of knowing anything or anyone at all. Even when what we are aware of is mistaken or quite wrong, it still makes a very big difference. Your awareness may not always be right, but it is always real. For a human *having life means being aware.* Since you have life, as you live your days from now on, you should expect to become aware of and find out many things that you do not know about now.

What You Are Is Unfinished: You Are Alive.

Whatever life is, you are too. Precisely what life is has not yet been agreed upon. The discussion continues in biology, where it is liveliest and loosest, and in philosophy, where it has lasted longest and everything is lengthy. Interest is mounting to determine when human life begins and ends, which is the same issue in another form. What is certain is that what life turns out to be, you and I will turn out to be also. You are it without having or doing anything at all. You could not get any closer to it than you already are even if you tried. It *is* you, and the closest we can ever come to anything is to be it.

With life we have the bond of *sameness*. What undermines it undercuts us, and when we fight for ourselves we do battle for it. Our pasts and futures are linked together. Where it came from, so did we, and we shall never go anywhere that it does not go along.

Life has taken three and a half billion years to form and fashion itself into you. Never before has life reached this far. Each day it perseveres, sets another record. Tucked away in every cell of your body are the instructions it has taken all those years to produce. It is a set of plans for bringing into being and keeping alive the particular individual you are, and this blueprint will continue to unfold your existence in an ongoing interaction with the environment that will not end until you die. This persistent striving, which you and I are, is life. For a human *being life means being alive.* More of you is yet to come. You are not finished until it is all over. And what it means to have *and* be life is another story altogether.

What You Do Unites Both: You Are Able to Act

A being that is alive and aware *does.* It is as simple as that. Whether it "moves about" or "just sits there" makes no real difference, for to a creature who is alive and aware everything is a deed. On the one hand we have the awareness that we live, while on the other hand we also live the awareness that we have. To say this in another way, we human beings are always, at one and the same time, embodying and enacting life.

Having and being come to life in doing. The last one consists of the first two in action. Doing is simply human life *in the act of occurring.* In all the world this is always and only found as a unique, unfinished, living expression of both what we have and what we are. It is understandable that certain individuals and sometimes whole cultures may stress one of these more than another.* But if this reaches the point of setting one up over the other two, then it paves the way for those prolific and all too familiar distortions of human life that make *having, being,* or *doing* an end in itself. Some common examples are: trying to amount to something by having things; trying to do everything so as not to miss anything; and trying to "comprehend all Being" but not be able to do anything with it (such as to use it to get one's stalled car going again). Such widespread maladies are attempts to capture the essence of life and win control by conquering it in part. Of course all of these finally fail and come up short, at death if not before. Because the only way a human being ever "captures" life is by living it to its fullest, which, of course, includes death too—and this fullness inevitably involves us in all three of the postures of human life.

In those rare and unforgettable moments when an earlier limit is gone beyond as our life reaches farther in some area than it ever did before, awareness and aliveness combine to create in us a new sense of what is humanly possible,

---

*The Orient, for example, has chosen to specialize more in the *sameness of being life,* as found in the contemplative and meditative achievements of the East; while the Occident, in its philosophic and scientific accomplishments, has chosen to give more attention to the *otherness of having life.* These two emphases, and their fruits over the centuries, are interpenetrating to an amazing degree in our time.

thereby giving us a new basis upon which to act. And when we begin to *do* that, new channels of life are opened to us that stretch to the horizon and beyond. For human beings life is also something done, and *doing life means being able to act.*

TO KNOW LIFE

To know human life is to participate fully in the having, being, and doing of one's life. Knowing means recognizing one's aliveness, awareness, and ability to act. This is not anything a person can do "once and for all" in life. Quite the contrary. Knowing life, at least that life which all humans share, is a never-ending act that lasts a lifetime.

It is this same act of knowing that we shall try to enter into now. Over the centuries, ways of knowing have been developed that are quite diverse. Such variety as this shows beyond all doubt that no one way works for everyone. Some prefer to use a diary or journal, others turn to silence and reflection, while many find dialog most helpful. But whether the word be mainly written, or thought, or spoken and interacted — or these in combination with still other forms — in order to be genuine knowing *it must touch upon all three aspects of human life: what we have, what we are, and what we do.*

The specific means we are about to use in our exploration of making a life were chosen because they aim at all three aspects. We can be sure that if knowing is truly this threefold act, then you and I must act in the same threefold way to participate in it.

Here is where we have reached a fork in the road and must decide to go down either the one path or the other. If we do not actually *do* something at this point, we will not move any further than we are right now. Why is that? If you just keep on reading, then you may keep on reading about and thinking about, and then maybe even talking about what you are reading and thinking about, and perhaps you will go so far as thinking about doing what you are talking about reading — all the while never moving half an inch beyond "aboutism." Is there not a huge difference between thinking about fear and being afraid, between talking about love and loving someone, and isn't this difference one that is big enough for us all to see? One does not find the whole by going part way. To know it you must plunge into your whole life, into all of it.

LOOK BEFORE YOU LEAP

A word of caution and encouragement before you take the plunge. Imagine a fisherman about to throw a net to bring in the biggest catch possible. No matter how skillfully he flings it, how far it flies, or widely it unfurls, there is no way for the fisherman to hurl out his net and haul himself in. We must recognize right here that it is impossible for us to completely contain ourselves within the nets of our awareness. We are more than our awareness can hold; that is, it works the other way around. We hold it, it does not hold us. As the fisherman holds his net, so we hold our awareness.

Perhaps you have heard about the centipede that loved running and the sheer momentum of moving his many legs about. One day, as he came across a worm, he stopped to give this legless marvel a closer look. The worm, also impressed, asked "How are you able to move all those legs at the same time?" "Wellll . . ." replied the centipede, "I never really thought about it before. Now, let me see . . . " He sat down to figure it all out. Before long, the centipede was so befuddled he could not go anywhere at all, for he could not think just how it was that he moved his legs. And the worm, who by this time had grown weary of waiting for an answer, and who didn't have a leg to stand on anyway, moved along. This is the word of caution before we embark.

The other story, which is the word of encouragement as we prepare to shove off from shore, is about Eliazar Hull, the captain of a whaling ship, who sailed from the ports of New England in the early 1800s. Eliazar (this name in Hebrew means "one whom God helps") was able to sail out farther, stay out longer, and, in that way, come back with a larger catch than anyone else. The owners of the fleet, seeking to insure their ships against damage or loss at sea, asked that all ship captains be schooled in the latest navigational techniques of the day, as the insuring companies had seen fit to require before granting policies to the owners.

When Eliazar arrived for training, the instructors, who had long since heard of his amazing sailing prowess, asked him how he was able to navigate the vast distances of such lengthy voyages without losing his way. Eliazar said, "I go up on deck at night, and I look at the stars, and I listen to the wind in the riggings, and I check the drift of the seas, and then I set my course." After completing his course in the science of navigation, Eliazar returned home and resumed his maritime vocation.

A while later it came time to see if the training had produced the desired results among all the captains. When they finally visited Eliazar, once again they asked how he navigated his great ship. "Exactly like you taught me," he responded to everyone's surprise, "I use the sextant to shoot the angle of the sun at midday. After fixing my longitude and latitude on the charts, I get out my compass and other instruments to plot my course. And then," he continued, "I go up on deck at night and I look at the stars, listen to the wind in the rigging, check the drift of the seas . . . and go back down to correct my calculations."

The tale of the worm and the centipede warns us not to limit our experience to our awareness alone, and the story of Eliazar Hull shows how marvelously deep and sagacious is the stuff of human experience. A simple sketch may help us bring these two observations together by showing:

(a) the relation of awareness to the rest of experience,
(b) the relation of experience to the rest of what there is,

and also serve as a reminder of these words of caution and encouragement.

ALL THE REST THERE IS

Experience

awareness

awareness + more

Experience + More

The Relation between Experience and Awareness— Awareness is contained in experience, and Experience is contained in all the rest of what there is.

EXPERIENCING THE THING ITSELF

Now it is time for you to take the matter in your own hands. Where this undertaking goes from here on is up to you.

As we said, whether it gets any further or remains where it is depends totally on whether you will choose to stay in aboutism or now move on into your own experiencing.

To Experience What You *Have*

SITUATION 1: Sit so you can easily see a watch or a clock without having to move. Then let your mind wander for one minute over the major periods of your life— where you were born, where you lived before you started school, where you went to grade school, then junior and senior high, where you moved or lived next, what you did after that . . . bringing it all up to the present.

Exploring Situation 1: Notice how much of your life you could see and feel in a single minute. That should help you grasp how fast and far experience can range in just sixty seconds. Every minute of your life experience has been busily moving on (even when you were asleep), and there are 1,440 of these experience spans in each day. How many days have you lived? You could total the figures, but can you start to fathom how incredibly immense and vast the experience record is which you carry around with you all the time and seldom notice? It is all there available to you, and sometimes little memory pieces turn up in your awareness without your knowing how they got there.

SITUATION 2: Think back to a time when as a child or youth you were struck with awe or wonder. Make an effort to recall such an experience from your early life. After you find one, look for another experience of wonder or awe which you have had as an adult, perhaps recently.

Exploring Situation 2: Use both of these experiences to sharpen the contrast and highlight your focus on the wonder and awe which you have come across in your life. It may have been quite thrilling, or very scary, or more than a little of both with some perplexity thrown in. How did you happen upon wonder as a child? How do you find that you meet it now, or do you no longer meet it at all? Wonder, awe, and even terror, arise out of some of our deepest experiences of life itself.

Many times people will look back with fondness on that wonder they experienced as a child and wish they could taste it again. Of course they cannot create it now, but they did not create it then either. It is futile and vain to try to generate wonder in order to experience more, though it is not at all uncommon to discover that opening more to one's experience can lead to a rebirth of wonder.

To Experience What You *Are*

TASK 1: Make yourself as comfortable as possible where you now are. Take time to pay attention to the body that you are, spending three or four seconds each on the various parts that will be mentioned. Since "head to toe" is the most commonly traveled path, let us give the feet a chance to be first.

Now — experience the soles of your feet (*remember*, you do not need to move in order to experience) . . . your heels . . . the backs of your legs up to the knee . . . the back of your legs on up to the buttocks . . . the buttocks and base of the spine . . . the lower back . . . middle back up to the shoulder blades . . . the back of your shoulders . . . the back of your arms from your shoulders down to your elbows . . . from your elbows down to your wrists . . . the back of your hands . . . your palms . . . the front of your arms from your wrists to your elbows . . . from your elbows up to your shoulders . . . the back of your neck . . . the back of your

head . . . the sides and top of your head . . . your hair
. . . your ears . . . your forehead . . . your brow . . . your
eyelids and eyelashes . . . your eyes . . . the bridge from
your brow on down your nose . . . your cheeks . . . the
whole facial mask . . . your upper lip . . . teeth, tongue,
throat, and tube to your lungs . . . your lower lip . . .
chin and jaw . . . your chest and rib cage . . . your stom-
ach . . . your abdomen and intestines . . . your hips and
pelvis . . . your genitals . . . the front of your legs from
your hips down to your knees . . . from your knees on
down to your ankles . . . your feet from your ankles
on to your toes . . . the tips of your toes . . . tips of your
fingers . . . tips of your ears . . . and the tip of your
nose. Now experience *all* of those, your total bodily
being all at once (you can easily do this in an instant).*

Exploring Task 1: All of the experience in your entire
life is found in one place and one place only: *in your
body.* You are not just anybody, you are *some*body. Anyone who wants to have any dealings with you must deal
with that particular body, for you are your body.

When you were still in the womb, only four weeks
old and a fifth of an inch long (which is about — long),
your tiny heart was pumping blood through the min-
uscule arteries and veins, bathing with nutrients
the developing brain, kidney, liver, and digestive
tract which you already possessed. Two months later
you were about as long as this:_____, and
your brain sent out impulses to keep your many organ
systems working in proper concert. Detectable reflexes
could be elicited from you; so you were already aware
way back then.

---

*Those who may, for whatever reason, be without a limb or body part
mentioned can still enter into each task, modifying them where necessary to access the ways and things they do experience as they go about
living their lives every day.

After your birth you kept on growing for another eighteen years or so, which is the longest growing span of any creature on earth (much longer than that of the whales and other larger mammals), in a swirl of somatic development made up of interaffecting skeletal, muscular, neural, psychobiochemical, and behavioral processes all aimed at equipping you for and contributing to your experience as a living human being. Become better acquainted with your body. Trust it. It is all you have to be anything with or to do anything through. It will never lie to you.

TASK 2: Take off your shoes or get a pair of your old ones. Check the soles and heels carefully to see how your feet strike the ground and for any other sign of how you throw your weight as you move about on your journey through the world.

Exploring Task 2: A walk is, in fact, a controlled fall. There is much speculation among anthropologists as to how and why we hominids ever got to our feet in the first place. We will probably never know for sure. Whatever the reason, standing puts a human being in a very precarious position, where the weight is delicately balanced and ready to topple at any moment. To *walk* is to quite deliberately knock the support out from underneath so that the whole structure tumbles earthward, using the muscles to arrest the mass in midair while heaving it all forward. It is an astonishing achievement.

But that isn't all. Standing exposes all of the vital organs, so that the creature is put in a state of at least mild general alert (as if the command center of the brain were sending a message, "Warning: all life-support systems threatened." This excites the cortex and places a host of neural pathways on ready. So, when we stand we have the heightened awareness of a creature at risk, and when we walk we transport our vulnerability through the world as an alert openness.

Task 3: Take note of any scars on your body, any chipped or broken bones, recalling whatever you are able to of any injuries in your life along with the events which led to them. Then think of any minor maladies that occasionally afflict you (e.g., colds; headaches; indigestion; pain from muscle strain, stress, and tension; aching limbs or joints), paying attention to their nature and frequency of occurrence. Recall any major illnesses or surgery, and what these did to your body.

TASK 4: When you take off your clothes before going to bed tonight, or at some other time soon that suits you, look at yourself in a full-length mirror. Since we experience ourselves primarily "from the inside out," we hardly ever look at our physical selves. Look at yourself long enough to get past the artificiality of the task to where you can catch some signs of the life of that unique human being you see before you.

Later, after you get into bed, before you go to sleep, try to think of two very different moments in your life: (a) when you felt the most awkward and embarrassed, and (b) when you felt the most "together," self-assured, or confident. How did you embody each of these antithetical states physically — in your head, neck and shoulders, trunk or torso, face, arms, and legs? Let your bodily memory work. Traces of these experiences are no doubt still there, still alive within you.

Exploring Task 3 and Task 4: The past of every individual leaves its mark upon his or her body. This is not only visible in the more obvious instances mentioned in Task 3, but also shows itself in the types of experiences touched upon in Task 4, though we are much more accustomed to keying on the memory content instead of the physical traces accompanying these in the body. That is why most of us have to work at such calisthenic-like tasks as these so we can learn to use some of the rest of what life has left us with. It is important not to rush these readings by looking for "insights." Just starting to attend to even the smallest connections between the events we experience, and their accompanying embodiments, will furnish you with more suggestive leads than you can possibly plumb or ever be able to follow to their conclusions.

To Experience What You *Do*

TASK 1: Notice your breathing. Let it be as it is without changing it—shallow or deep, rushed or calm. Pay attention to it long enough to make the following observations:

> (1) Follow a complete cycle from inhalation through exhalation. Is one longer? Do you have a slight preference for one or another, so it seems to feel a little "better" or more natural?
> (2) Look to see if you can notice any pauses. Do you? If so, where are they; after inhalation, exhalation, or after both?

Exploring Task 1: Some people inhale for a longer duration than they exhale, and others do the opposite. Some find both of these actions to be fairly equal in length. Others have pronounced pauses in the places mentioned, while the breathing of still others does not seem to contain much pause at all.

Our breathing indicates when changes occur in both our physical and mental states (if the two can be spoken of as being "two" at all), and can serve as a kind of barometer of one's general experience. *Note:* When you started to notice your breathing, if you felt that it changed, then you have a concrete example of how experience differs from awareness. You would not have been able to know it changed if you had not already experienced what it was before you chose to make yourself aware of it.

The renowned biologist Edmund Sinnott once commented that when it comes to breathing, he would defy anyone to clearly draw the line between instinct and behavior. You and I have a considerable role in determining that specific way in which we "normally" breathe.

TASK 2: Tonight, or on some evening in the near future that is typical of your regular routine, watch as you go through your usual way of "getting ready for bed." If you have no standard way, then heed the randomness with which you regularly end a day. Continue this gentle monitoring as you awake the following morning, and learn how you choose to go about beginning a new day.

Exploring Task 2: Some people have a highly elaborate ritual for ending the day. They gradually start to "unwind" through some light activity, or by making preparations for the next day (e.g., setting the table for breakfast, getting tomorrow's wardrobe laid out, etc.). Then they may put milk out for the cat, take the dog for a walk, read for a while or watch television, turn down the bed, and, when they are really ready, crawl into their favorite position to go to sleep.* Other individuals end the day abruptly or suddenly, falling asleep on the couch, the floor, in a chair, or anywhere.

---

*The act of going to sleep furnishes us with yet another clear example of the significant difference between awareness and experience. We enter sleep through experience. There is no way to reach sleep through awareness, as all insomniacs can testify.

The next morning some of us arise vigorous and alert, exercising or jogging for a few miles, or slip effortlessly into the day with quiet meditation and breathing exercises, or, just as simply and profoundly, sitting on the patio or at the kitchen table with a cup of coffee, just "taking it all in" or reading the morning newspaper. There are still others who repeatedly begin the day with a mountainous reluctance, having to muster the energy of a salmon making its way upstream at spawning time, and who know it will be no earlier than mid-morning before they are "really awake," or maybe mid-afternoon, and, for a few, it will be evening before they are "at their best."

Bringing Task 1 and Task 2 together: See if you can now reap the benefits of your explorational efforts and uncover any similarities between how you handle your inhaling and exhaling, for example, and how you generally "take in" and "give out" things in your life. Of course we all do both, but is one easier or harder for you than the other? Do you regard one as any more important?

In what you were able to bring to light about how you end and begin your days, can you glean anything from how you generally go about handling endings and beginnings in your life? Do you stretch them out or prefer to keep them short and sudden? If so, which one: things ending or things beginning? Do you like to start something only after something else is finished, or do you tend more to "never finish what you start," or are you simply "finished before you start"? Are hellos as easy as goodbyes? Can you say Yes as easily as you can say No? Do you — and to yourself as well as to other people?

As you discover more and more that acts as specific as your breathing and as general as how you may end or begin your day both hold signs of your individual will and personal intent, then you are well on your way to making deeper and more rewarding discoveries. These discoveries, and others like them, might be helpful for you to know and act on in the future. They might even grow to illuminate additional aspects of your life. When any such learnings are genuine, their discovery is never forced or strained. The more you open yourself to your own experiencing, the more effortlessly such learning and knowing is likely to occur, and you will see with increasing certainty that in all you do there is something as recognizably unique as your own fingerprint.

THE LIFE THAT IS YET TO COME

As you open up to more of your experience, your existence opens to more life. To start experiencing more amounts to the same thing as starting to live more. Yet when you do this, events do not all of a sudden arise and pass before you fully uniformed and decorated like marching bands and decorated floats in the grand parade of life which you had somehow been missing out on. Not at all. At first, this entering into the rest of one's experience comes as a wondering about life once more, an attitude not all that far from finding things rather puzzling. It is only when one stays with this for a while longer that it begins to become something akin to wonder again, the wonder you had in your youth when life was far too big for you to try to control, something you never asked for and would never have dreamed you could understand, but still something you knew you somehow had a stake in and were involved in up to the hilt, and therefore expected to be finding out a whole lot more about.

Regardless of how open any of us are, there is always more life yet to come. We forget this. In the case of our own life, we think we know most of all there is to know, at least all that is worth knowing. That is why we habitually underestimate our experience and underexperience our life. Moving to break this long-standing habit, our first discovery is that there is more to life, starting with our own, than we ever believed was there. And this is where we truly start to wonder again, to experience life once more, and to begin to know.

You and I and everyone else have the capacity to do this, to experience the life we enact and embody. Through this you can know that what you have, do, and are, is life. Through it too you will know that more is yet to come. In opening the door to this more, one finds that it opens out onto the world.

Getting on with It

What do we have but life?
What is it for but to live?
When shall we live it more than now?
Where will we live it more than here?
How can we live it unless we act?
Who is able to act more than you?
What do you have but life?
What is it for but to live?

·3·

IN A TIME LIKE THIS

> We are in a better frame of mind today to conceive a natural philosophy than of any time in the last three hundred years. This is because the recent findings in human biology have given a new direction to scientific thought, a shift from the general to the individual, for the first time since the Renaissance opened the door into the natural world.   —*J. Bronowski*

YOU WEREN'T BORN YESTERDAY

You were not born yesterday. We have both been making a life for years. For us to try to deal with this is like coming in on a movie after it has already started. The film cannot very well be rolled back and replayed from the beginning, and no one can really catch you up on everything that has taken place so far — not without your missing what is going on at the moment. The whole thing just keeps right on playing. All you can do is pick it up from where you came in and get into it as best you can. There is no other way.

This is a very big order, to say the least — as big as life itself. What makes it possible though is that life is always distinct, definite, and, at least with human life, even personal. How so? It is a matter of someone somewhere doing

24

something sometime. In a word, life as it really occurs is always specific. Specificity is one of the famous facts of life. When it comes to human life then, if we are willing to deal with the specifics, the actual *someone* who is *somewhere* doing *something* at *sometime,* then we can begin to lay hands on and take hold of our lives.

A powerful current within us runs in the opposite direction however, away from all particularity. How strange it is that life is so very specific and our approaches to it are so general. By its sheer size the general seems to have the edge in appearing so much more important and worthwhile. It looks like the most direct route to what life is all about and the surest shortcut to certainty. After all, why bother with little subjective truths when there is a gigantic objective one to be had? And that might lead us on to an even bigger and better one, and so on. How puny is the personal alongside the grand universal; and the less we see of ourselves, the grander we seem to become. Thus it is that we learn to leapfrog after life, loving to lunge toward what looms ever larger.

Furthermore, the language of leapfrogging is so global and cosmically impersonal that it lulls us into thinking we have transcended the self altogether. But at bottom all this is merely the same old timeworn attempt to make ourselves more than we really are. Nothing exposes smallness so quickly and completely as its hunger for bigness.

Of course this attempt is totally in vain. Sooner or later it falters, flops, and finally fails — at death, if not before, where the whole charade collapses into a humble pile of unmistakably human particulars. The irony is that in doing all this we lose the very thing we seek as we throw away with one hand what we are reaching out for with the other. For when we turn up our nose at and turn our backs on the sights, sounds, smells, and sense of our very own specificity, then we miss all that is green and grand, inheriting in its place the broadly bland, and lose the life of ourselves, our souls and bodies.

WHO, WHAT, WHEN, WHERE, HOW, AND WHY

We are not here to do what has already been done.
— R. Henri

Specifics make all the difference in the world. Think what a big difference the following things make: the body one comes into being with; where one is born and grows up; the language one speaks; what one eats, drinks, breathes, thinks, and does; and the time one lives in. To treat our subject — making a life — we must keep this fact of specificity constantly before us in the image of human life as *an actually existing somebody who is always doing something somewhere at sometime.*

We dealt with some of the *who, what,* and *how* of your life in Chapter 2. So let us now go into some of your life's *when* and *where.*

RECOLLECTION OF A WHEN AND WHERE: Try to recall your first or one of your earliest days at school. Give yourself at least four or five minutes to do this.

Exploring the Recollection: It is surprising how vivid such memories as these can be. Often these pictures stand out in the mind into the last years of life. People in their nineties are often able to recall what they wore, how they got there, what the room or weather was like, something others said or did, or what happened when they got back home.

Try to get a real taste of how different life was back then. It might have been in the days before television, during the time of radio when people used more of what came through their ears than their eyes to paint the pictures in their minds. Or maybe it was after that, but before the atomic and nuclear age; before man set foot on the moon or traveled in space; before computers and pocket calculators, or the proliferating sights and sounds of increasingly sophisticated electronic games.

The way life was back then is not at all the way it is now. We can go home again, but only to the places of our own past—not the time. Time flows in only one direction. With it there is never any going back. This makes the *when* different from all the other specifics of life in this way: *it is the one specific we all share in simultaneously.* Since life is all the while moving on, at any one point in time it is unlike what it was before or will be after. To know this specific we must look more closely at life as we find it in the present age. As we delve into this now, we shall find that it brings us face to face with a mammoth event occurring in our time which affects us all.

THINGS AREN'T WHAT THEY USED TO BE

> *The present stage may be looked upon as a kind of new beginning: old laws, rules, or values are no longer considered adequate, and a whole new system of relationships, values, and rules needs to be developed and accepted as more appropriate to the presently changing circumstances.* — Jonas Salk

In the 1960s the words of two people were picked up, read, and quoted by millions of others around the world. One was a paleontologist priest and man of science, who spent years studying the evolution of life on earth, and whose digging into the past made him, he said, "a pilgrim of the future." His name was Teilhard de Chardin, and this is what he said about the times:

> There is now incontrovertible evidence that mankind has just entered upon the greatest period of change the

world has ever known. The ills from which we are suffering have had their seat in the very foundations of human thought. But today something is happening to the whole structure of human consciousness. A fresh kind of life is starting . . . The task before us now, if we would not perish, is to build the earth.

The other one was a frizzy-haired young man, barely in his twenties, who was known far and wide as Bob Dylan. As he did with most everything else back then, he put it in his own way into a song.

> Come gather 'round people
> wherever you roam.
> Admit that the waters
> around you have grown.
> If you don't start swimming
> then you'll sink like a stone.
> For the times they are a-changing.

What was hard to believe about this was that two individuals unknown to each other and so unalike — a French scientist and priest whose career had just come to an end, and a folk-rock musician whose career had just begun — should turn out to be saying essentially the same thing about what they saw taking place in the lives of human beings everywhere in the world.

In the 1960s just about everybody around could tell something was happening, which in itself is rather remarkable, but no one was able to say quite what it was. Children around eleven years of age expressed it mostly as "things being different from what they used to be" (with those in their teens experiencing it as an especially heady mixture of both coming of age and the coming of an age), while those under ten were bound to take all of this as pretty much "the way things are."

As the "something happening" grew, so too did the attention paid to it, leading some to say that the attention itself was what was causing "it." Television, magazines, newspapers, books, and even scholarly academic journals, all cranked up and cranked out theories to explain what was taking place. It was "the generation gap," "the age of anxiety," "the pursuit of loneliness," "the youth culture," "the making of a counterculture," "the greening of America," and on and on. As historians, philosophers, economists, scientists, theologians, poets, and specialists of every stripe were pressed into the role of commentator, some willingly and some reluctantly, we began to hear of "the global village," "future shock," "the great ascent," the "technocratic society," and of "neoromanticism," "between two ages," a "pre-Reformation period," "the dawning of the Age of Aquarius," and other emerging concepts. A few of these interpretations were quite profound and illuminated this or that feature of what was happening. But "it" gained so in size, speed, and spread, that it soon outgrew, outran, and outdistanced all explanations, opening a huge gap between its staggering immensity on the one side, and our not-as-great conceptions of it, with the result that many of these silently tumbled into the ever-widening void, never to be seen or heard of again. Meanwhile, it kept right on, getting bigger, moving faster, and spreading farther. About all we could tell was that whatever *it* might turn out to be, it was without a doubt something big, broad, and basic.

WHAT IS HAPPENING IN OUR TIME

To explore this "it" would indeed make a book by itself. Many books have already been written on this subject alone, and hundreds of others surely will be written in the time to come. (One of the first and best of these is *The Meaning of the 20th Century*, New York, Harper & Row, written by Kenneth Boulding in 1964 and still well worth reading.) It is appropriate here simply to mention "its" main features so we can better see the crucial bearing it has on the business of making a life.

It is as if humankind the world over woke up one morning and decided to change its mind. *A shift has begun in the human species. Our experience of life and the universe has changed.*

In *The Survival of the Wisest,* a book which deserves serious attention, Jonas Salk sets forth a provocative explanation of what is taking place in human evolution. An epochal transition occurs when any species reaches its "point of inflection," a distinct point that divides its life into a definite before and after of two unalike eras which Salk names Epoch A and Epoch B. Salk is convinced that humankind has reached this most critical point and is presently passing through it. Such a mammoth transition in the life of a species is understandably neither smooth, automatic, nor irresistible. Though it involves everyone, it does not include everyone, hence the book's disturbing title.*

What Salk describes happens in most all living species. Why should it not happen in our own? If he is right about what is taking place, then human life is certainly altering in unprecedented ways. Some will surely say, "But human life is *always* changing! So how can you say that one period is more special than any other?" But this attitude glosses over some exceptionally important differences. For example, we now have the technology to directly intervene in the life process and intentionally alter its design, thereby bringing into being forms of life altogether new and dif-

---

*Salk, drawing from his knowledge of molecular biology and other fields, elaborates his points with graphs, charts, and tables which must be viewed directly to be properly understood. Much of his conceptualizing about human life is fresh and goes beyond spurious dichotomies that lead to such pointless debates as "heredity vs. environment," etc. He outlines a new discipline called "metabiology," which builds upon all the existing scientific disciplines to push the frontiers beyond those biological processes we do understand, on toward those even larger functions of human life and being which we do not. (*Survival of the Wisest,* New York: Harper & Row, 1973)

ferent.* Never before in all the three and a half billion years of life on this planet has this been possible; but it is possible now — in fact we are already doing it. An event of this magnitude cannot legitimately be dismissed as insignificant. In the present work with interferons we have only begun to get an inkling of that mixture of risks and rewards to which this one feature of our time alone can lead.

WHAT IT MEANS

First: If human nature is shifting, then human life has changed. To be alive today is to be part of it. It is as fundamental as that. You might welcome this or regret it, but the simple fact is that neither you, nor I, nor anyone else alive today, will be able to avoid, remove, or escape this fact.

Nature is not separate from our life, and our life is not separate from what we experience. Whatever is happening in human life today can be found right there in the backyards of our own experiencing.

Second: We can expect to see more of a special kind of craving, an *experience hunger,* roaming the land in search of the most primary, vigorous, substantive experiencing open to human beings. At its deepest this is not thrill-seeking (though, to be sure, it can degenerate into that). Instead, it is an attempt to find the edges of things once more, to make one's way further on by plumbing the depths, scaling the heights, and soaring the heavens in order to learn the

---

* Breakthroughs in Recombinant DNA or "gene splicing," made possible by the work of Crick and Watson (building on that of Chargaff, Franklin, Wilkins, and several others) in unraveling the DNA double helix in 1953, is only one of the bigger changes of our time. Other formative factors have arisen in worldwide demographic and economic changes, recent fossil finds, current brain research, present space probes, and major alterations in human institutions, sexual roles, and life-styles — to name a few.

limits and set new boundaries. It is all a reexploration of experience, and reexperiencing of the world.

Third: The future, so often spoken of, is here. It is not at its peak but has fully dawned. The significance of the recent past lies in what we have lived our way into, none too gracefully in fits and starts; while that of the present, the near and even distant future, surely lies now in what we do — or don't do. The New Age has arrived. Our task, yours and mine, is to enter it.

WHY IT IS SO HARD TO SEE

It is little wonder that all this took us so completely by surprise. Like all of the better-known periods of change in human history, its very nature served to keep it hidden.* Our species-old habit is to proceed through life by using the established method of the tried and true. We normally make our way along by using the known to explain the unknown. This wisdom, which serves us so well when it comes to everything else, draws up short when it comes across the totally new. Since what was happening was something we had never experienced before, of course we had nothing to compare it to, and so we did one of three things:

(1) We concluded that there really was not anything to it after all.

(2) We boiled it down to something else that had happened before and thought it was not anything new.

(3) We stood apart from both of these two groups,

---

*As John Gardner so aptly expressed it: "The historic innovation looks exciting in the history books, but if one could question those who lived at the time, the typical response would be neither 'I opposed it' nor 'I welcomed it,' but 'I didn't know it was happening.'" (*Self-Renewal: The Individual and the Innovative Society,* New York: Harper, 1965, p. 29) unable to join either one, and were left with a nameless sense of something that could neither be seen nor shaken off.

At the outset, the hordes in the first two groups far outnumbered the few who found themselves in the third. With time, however, the last group began to grow while the other two sank in a gradual decline, and it was in this same unformed party that a tiny band arose of individuals who were the first to sense and send out the signal that something new was happening.

That is how it was back when all this first began, before we knew there was no way out of it but through it, and that "it" was something that had to be undergone in order to be understood (Why do we humans try so hard to explain our experiences away instead of having them?).

Since that time we have made enough headway through this to know it from our own experience. We can see clearly now that it is all of a piece, and that what is needed most is not a way out but a way on.

FROM NOW ON

We are continually living a solution of problems that reflection cannot hope to solve. — J. H. Van den Berg

The present is not drawing up to the future and connecting with it like a railroad car, enabling us to step into it the way one moves to the car ahead on a train. No. The future comes out of the present. What will soon come to be is largely an extension or working out of things already in motion. Indeed, you and I are preparing for the future right now by molding and shaping those pieces of it — namely, our lives — which are for us alone to make. "What the future holds," therefore, is not an ethereal matter at all, but a matter to be taken into our own hands.

Why we do not experience life more this way is because

we generally fail to see experience as something we have a hand in creating. We tend to see it more as something that descends upon us or simply happens. To see it as something we do without doubt have a hand in making prompts us to at least start looking around for the tiller, and then to reach out to grasp it, to move it this way or that to see if it really is true that one can steer experience enough to sail in life for oneself.

Human experience, which is the only thing we have all of life through, is much too big and far too broad to belong to any one academic discipline, profession, or special field of study; for it embraces art, science, religion, history, philosophy, politics, economics — in short, each and every facet of human culture. Any approach to it that is to be valid and genuine must include not only all of these, but it must also do justice to the very ordinary day-in-and-day-out events in the lives of people as well. Human experience plainly belongs to us all, so it is a matter on which either everyone is an expert, or no one is.

In the grand undertaking that faces humanity now, or even in that much smaller venture which is the subject of this book, we cannot rule out any of these fundamental vocabularies, these chosen ways of viewing life and speaking about it, which humans have thus far seen fit to develop. We must attempt to remain open to all of these tongues, as well as to the language of the commonplace, customary, and everyday — and, what is even more, we must be prepared to develop new ones as well.

If many of us alive today can accomplish this, then humankind could well make discoveries about life which hitherto were unknown and unknowable. Furthermore, if we who choose to make this attempt should link together, we would most likely witness a renaissance as significant as any that has occurred in all human history — and which *if we persist* may yet prove to be greater. From this point on it should be crystal clear that as we go on with our venture

of making a life, you and I are also playing our own parts
in that larger venture which is confronting all humankind
in our time.

The Me I've Not Yet Been

What used to be
is no longer.
The way I saw
I'll never see again.

Yet something there
grows ever stronger,
helping to make real
the me I've not yet been.

·4·

MAKING A LIFE

LOOK AT WHAT YOU'VE DONE

So far we have aimed at *using* your experience and awareness. Now what we must do is *look at* them both. Then we can use them to their fullest from here on as we resume our exploration into the life you are making.

When some people make the discovery that experience is both bigger than and contains awareness, they can be misled into reasoning that awareness must then only be something to get beyond. So they constantly keep springing into those places beyond awareness lying at the very rim of experience, trying to continually ride "the cutting edge." This might mend communing but it mars communicating. It is not difficult at all to get to where one feels "beyond words." But when one also gets beyond all experienced meaning — and stays there — then, ultimately, one goes mad. In reality these people are choosing to expand one part of their experience and to atrophy in another — therefore it is not an increase at all. Whatever truly extends experience expands the range of awareness too because it enlarges the terrain into which it can then move. After all, the greats are not those who merely fly to new heights, but those who are able to also return to the ground, where the rest of us live, and then take off to soar again.

Surely you have heard of "not being able to see the forest

for the trees." That is exactly where we would all be if we had no awareness: we would all be too busy experiencing trees to discover they were part of something called a forest. Awareness is extremely important in its own right and comes in very handy; it is only because of it that we do not have to go into every forest to know something about trees. So let us take two steps back, now, and try to get a better look at what making a life involves and is all about.

THE SIGN OF A LIFE — READING THE SIGNS

Human personality is not a ready-made object: man creates it especially in knowing himself, for "self" is primarily an act.
—N. Berdyaev

Experience is *life in the act of making sense.* It is life moving in thought, word, and deed to make sense and read the signs of everything it comes across. Human experience is the mark, the very first indication, of human life. It is a reality that always has these three aspects to it: the *experiencer* (the *who* of experience), the *experienced* (the *what* of experience), and the *experiencing* (the act of experience that unites the who and what in a meaningful whole). The one word "experience" is made up of and can be broken down into all three of these.

Human experience, then, is not something that just happens — it is made. Once it occurs, life is no longer merely lived out but *experienced;* and at that same moment human life begins, continuing on up to its very end. We keep right on making sense of whatever we come across, all the while living that sense which we make, and this is precisely the way we come to build our lives.

THE SENSE OF LIFE — COMING TO TERMS

Now it is at the heart of my present that I find the meaning of those presents which preceded it, and that I find the means of

understanding others' presence in the same world; and it is in the actual practice of speaking that I learn to understand.
— Merleau-Ponty

Let us now come to terms with human experience.* You are already familiar from earlier sections with the distinction between *awareness* and *experience,* which was diagrammed on page 13 both in relation to one another and to the world. Picture human experience, if you will, as a globe — like the earth with its north and south poles. Just as it is possible to travel to one pole or another, so can a person move at will from the experience end of the pole all the way to the awareness end at the other, or chance to stand at any moment somewhere in between. This is done by choosing to focus one's attention on the *experiencer field* at the one end, or on the *experienced field* at the other. We have referred to these as *the who of experience* and *the what of experience* respectively. Some refer to these as "subjective" and "objective," which is all right if one remembers they are nothing more than opposite ends of the same pole, which we humans are moving our attention back and forth along at will each and every moment in some act of experiencing.

Next, we must recognize that human experience has edges and an end to it, a boundary where it leaves off and something else begins. In other words, we are saying that human experience isn't everything.† Let us call that area within these limits the *context.* Experience can only happen in a context, in some specific set of meanings, assumptions,

---

*A glossary of the key terms used here and elsewhere will be found in the back of the book.

† The three greatest realities I know are God or the holy, the universe, and human experience. But the significance of the last one lies in the fact that for all human creatures, the first two are known only through it.

and attitudes, which is why every experience always means something, even experiences of meaninglessness.

Across time an individual develops a fairly pronounced overall context in which life is consistently experienced. We will call this the *life-defining context*. Occasionally this basic context is intruded upon in striking ways that lead to profound and lasting changes later on, and we shall call this *context-puncture*.

Whenever context-puncture occurs, an individual meets *the more* of life, which is the rest of what there is to a person outside his or her *self-picture*. The "self-picture" and the "more" make up the *self*, which is that unique and living whole that embodies and enacts all the contexts, contents, and experiencings of a particular human being. Outside the self, of course, there are other creatures, other selves, other things, other worlds, and that grand immensity beyond even these which we shall refer to here as the *More*.

Those moments in life when a person experiences the more, and begins to know some of the rest of what he or she is, are special. These are often accompanied by a vivid sense of being "all there." Let us call this *presence*. And, as sometimes also happens, if two people experience presence simultaneously and exchange it, then let us call such experiencing as this an *engagement*. When two or more engagements take place, interaffecting all of those involved, we shall term such an occurrence an *event*.

These are some of the basic words we shall use in our exploration of human experience. To learn what the marks of experience are, is to begin to read the signs of life.

THE STUFF OF LIFE — MOLDING THE CLAY

> *In any living thing this organized system . . . this coordinating mechanism which regulates behavior . . . is the same as that which coordinates all other vital activities, notably those of development and function.* — E. Sinnott

There is a background, foreground, aboveground, and belowground to all human experience. These make up the
stuff of life.

The *Background* of Life: the times, language, and givens one can't get away from

What there in fact *is*, what *is* given, is my coexistence
with things, that absolute event — a self *in* its
circumstances.   — Ortega y Gasset

Nobody grows up in a vacuum. They always live at a
particular time in history. Volcanic eruptions and earth-
quakes, political revolutions and social upheavals, scientific
and technological inventions — these and other factors
bring realities into being at one time and move them away
at others. Also, an individual grows up in the setting of a
specific language, culture, and cluster of influencing relationships. All of these combined form the background of
a life. This background changes across time, but it is always
there, and it is impossible to extract oneself from it. Much
of the context of our experience comes from the setting
given us as the background of our lives.

The *Belowground* of Life: itchings, urges, longings and stirrings

*A mysterious power that all may feel, and no philosophy can
explain.*   — Goethe

The belowground is the movement at the depth or source
of a life. Like most sources, it is often overlooked and easily
underestimated. Some people have a lot to say about it, so
it has been given a great number of names, but most people
know more about its names than they know about it. Regardless of what it is called, though, every single human
being has it; and after all our thinking, talking, reading,

and wondering about it, it remains there — seeming big now, or small, but always *alive,* something for one to make something of.

It may take years for us to finally stumble upon it. When we do, we may label it as something foreign. Then we will see it mainly as an "it," which makes it like some foreigner whose rights and whereabouts are to be only within those limits we prescribe. Of course it heeds no such limits but keeps on moving, because our life is more a spring than a stagnant pond, until it eventually spills around the edges of our comprehension to well up within us as urges, longings, itches, and stirrings of every kind. Because it is our own "more," yet not recognized or called so, we thus become strangers to our own vitality. Then when it moves or stirs we experience it as some invasion from without, a threatening intrusion upon our native soil we somehow sensed would one day surely come.

On the other hand, we might label it as something familiar, as feelings and fascinations that may leave us either overwhelmed or pleasantly whelmed from time to time. Such teasing and tingling titillations are the stuff of which attractions and affairs are often made — when one "falls in love" with those qualities in another person that bear a suspiciously striking resemblance to the yet undiscovered dimensions of oneself. When the discovery is eventually made that the stirrings of one's long-submerged self have surfaced, then a truly new way of living can indeed begin — which, of course, is exactly where most affairs come to an end. Whatever popular sentiment may lead one to say, feel, or think at such moments, each one involved must then choose and pay the cost of either going along with the old or getting on with the new.

Whether an individual meets the belowground as foreign or familiar, *it will stir and move;* and we wonder what has come over us, when all the while the issue is what is taking place under us, there where it seems the ground has been pulled out from beneath our feet, but which is the very place where we must find our footing or fall.

When we recognize the belowground for what it is, come to know it, claim it, and express it, then the rest of what we are begins to connect us with the rest of what there is. For "it" is our own more. It can never be lost — for where else can it go? —it can only not be found. Much of what strikes, stirs, or moves us powerfully comes from the belowground of our lives.

The *Aboveground* of Life: dreams, demons, things unnamed and unknown

Toto, I've a feeling we're not in Kansas anymore.
— Dorothy in *The Wizard of Oz*

There are some experiences we never find good words for. Dreams can take our souls soaring, or leave us with such unspeakable sadness or unfathomable serenity, which even though inexplicable is nevertheless so exquisitely clear, that they surpass many other such experiences in our lives and continue to stand out in our memory. They become like a painting one happens upon in the side gallery of some museum. The artist is unknown to us, but the subject and treatment of it seizes our attention and will not let it go, though its rendering has meanings of which we are not altogether sure. That is how it often is with dreams.

And there are visions too, some sought and some not, much grander and longer lasting than dreams, and that can be seen when one is wide awake. Then too, what might a demon be? Or the splendid magic of an unforgettable moment on some starry summer night? And for centuries millions of people have spoken of an abyss, that out of which the bottom keeps dropping.

Whatever these experiences are or may turn out to be, whatever we may choose to call this watchamacallit, the fact remains that in such acts human beings are experiencing something. It is still a most interesting and open question whether or not the same type of experiences are open to all. Is everyone able to experience as Columbus did, or Joan of Arc, or Einstein, or Homer, or as Spartacus, Moses, Socrates, Buddha, Muhammad, Shakespeare, or Jesus — or an astronaut . . . a clown . . . or someone living down the street? How much do you suppose your neighbor has experienced of what you have, and vice versa?

Simply because you or I may not have experienced such things so far is certainly no indication that we never shall. Life is something that for you and me is not yet used up. We may get it into our minds we have finished with it, but it clearly has not finished with us or we would not still be here. There is always at least the outside chance that we will yet meet up with something considerably more than we ever met before, for much of life is still up in the air.

The *Foreground* of Life:
peaks, pits, plateaus, and all of the wanderings and wonderings in between

> *His real life is led in his head, and is known to none but himself . . . it and its volcanic fires that toss and boil, and never rest night or day. These are his life, and they are not written, and cannot be written.* — Mark Twain

All human experience finally funnels into the foreground of an actual someone's life. One and all, rich and poor, old and young, black, white, red, yellow, and brown alike — we go through the motions of life with longings, urges, stirrings, whatever their kind, have our dreams, meet the unknown and unnamed in our unique ways — and all of this becomes the foreground of a human life.

The foreground is the lived experience of an individual across time. It is the thread that runs throughout a life and on which all its experiences are strung. We experience more than we remember, and because of the way our mind works, we remember "more," or a little differently, than we experience.*

Whatever happens to or for any individual, and whatever he or she may or may not later recall of it, that person in every case experiences *something*. This something comprises the foreground of that person's life, and it always hooks up with and joins itself to the background, beneathground, and aboveground of his or her life.† All four of these grounds color in the overall context within which an individual experiences life.

THE SIGN, SENSE, AND STUFF OF LIFE —*EXPERIENCING IT ALL*

A proper approach . . . should take into account the implications of the individual's situation and interaction with the

---

*The *foreground* should not be taken to be "consciousness," which has proven to be a most inexact and unfortunate term because it suggests that the other three grounds of a life are to be taken as somehow "unconscious." This reasoning misleads many to assume that human beings somehow do not, indeed *cannot,* manage to reach or experience the greater or most significant levels of their lives — a mistaken notion which, though derived mostly from a definition, is unhappily still widespread.

† As Mark Twain once wrote, "For many years I believed I remembered helping my grandfather drink his whiskey toddy when I was six weeks old, but I do not tell about that anymore now; I am grown old and my memory is not as active as it used to be. When I was younger I could remember anything, whether it happened or not; but my faculties are decaying now and soon I shall be so I cannot remember any but the things that never happened. It is sad to go to pieces like this but we all have to do it." (*The Autobiography of Mark Twain,* ed. by Charles Neider, New York: Harper & Row, 1959.)

The workings of memory, of which we still know very little, can not be gone into here. Generally, when we put something in memory we quite literally *re-member* it, not unlike the way we store things in a freezer. What we then take out later are the cuts and pieces into which we packaged the original experience.

environment, the plasticity of the brain both to transient and to long-term changes, and the transgenerational effects imposed by environmental alterations. — Steven Rose

The *physical aspect* of life, of course, is the body. The total experience environment has three main realms, which are associated with though not limited to the forebrain (think-

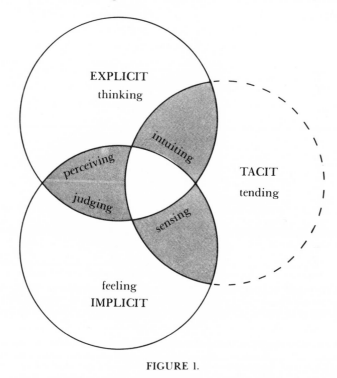

FIGURE 1.

The Embodiment of Human Experience*

---

*See Glossary and Locator of the back of the book for an exanded treatment of these terms and concepts.

ing), the midbrain (feeling), and the hindbrain (tending)*
functions of the human central nervous system.

The three primary experience realms have their own cor-
responding type of meaning and each gives rise to a basic
human experience-state. These three basic states can mix
and intermingle to form still other states (such as sensing,
intuiting, judging, and perceiving). This is comparable to
the way the primary colors combine to form the other colors. But whether simple or complex, every human experience is essentially a whole, with a particular meaning-

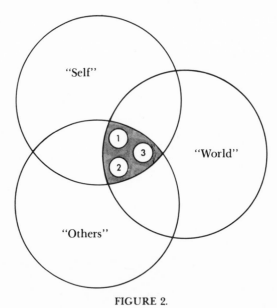

FIGURE 2.

The Enactment of Human Experience

---

* *Tending* in both senses: as in tending to a garden, and as in tending
toward the future.

quality of its own, much like we experience green as green itself rather than perceiving it as a mixture of blue and yellow.

Every experience-state of a human being affects and is affected by the body as a whole. *All human life and experience is embodied.*

The *contextual aspect* of life is where sense is being made at the moment. It is the life-defining context mentioned earlier, which contains the individual's picture of "Self," "Other," and "World."

Self, Other, and World are placed in quotes to emphasize that they are the pictures one holds of these things. Refer to figure 2. The numbers indicate the possibility of the human organism choosing to move or orient itself (1) more in its picture of itself, (2) more in its picture of other beings, (3) more in the picture it has of everything else.

A person's experience of the present is always affected by experience of the past. The three smaller contexts represent all material and information stored in memory. *All human life and experience has significance.*

The *temporal aspect* of life is visible in its duration, or in the time it always takes to happen. There is no avoiding the fact that even the very tiniest piece of experience is still a segment of time. This durational aspect writ large is that same dynamic process of a human life going through its beginning, middle, and end. At any moment of human life an individual is always spending time reaching into some greater or lesser part of the whole environment of human experience.

The act of making the sense of the moment can easily be shown by placing the life-defining context in the overall experience environment (as FIGURE 3 indicates a person involved at the moment in thinking). The dotted line in the drawing depicts the temporal yet-to-be-unfolded aspect of human life.

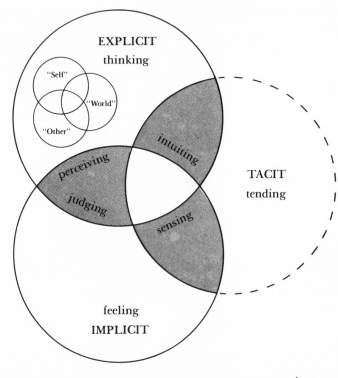

FIGURE 3.

The Embodiment and Enactment of Human Experience

At any moment, more than all you have been and done, you are what you are becoming. *All human life and experience is enacted.*

A MATTER OF WORDS

For wordplay is thoughtplay; and play can be a dead-serious business, the rhythmic awareness of the unimagined possibilities of an ever-renewing, dying, resurgent nature. To find one's way back to the clear and undefiled spring from which language flows is granted a few. — Erwin Chargaff

Human life and experience, with its substance and sense, is *a matter of words.* If this seems to make too little of it, it is only because we think too little of words. Words are deeds, something done; and deeds are words, or things that mean something.* We imagine thought and action as being far apart, though they are really inseparable. Think of food, and the mouth can water. Think you left the oven on at home, or lost your wallet or pocketbook, or forgot to pick up someone waiting for you — and watch your body send the alarm and spring to alert. When we find out later it was all a mistake, it is still exceedingly clear how instantaneously and totally the body wrenches at something that is "only an idea."

Moreover, when someone says "I love you," and means it, words and deed merge — and something happens in those two lives and in the world. As important an issue as trust, for example, is largely a matter of being taken at one's word. We humans live by our words.† So when we don't know what to say, we also usually don't know what to do. To find one's words again is to find one's way again. When all else fails and comes to no avail, try saying what you mean — and see what happens.

---

*In biblical Hebrew the word for *word* (dabar) means both things spoken (or heard, thought, or written) and things done. This unity is found in the creation story where the utterances of God bring all creation into being, in "Man shall not live by bread alone, but by every word . . .", and "In the beginning was the Word . . ." and in other passages too numerous to mention.

† To illustrate, suppose someone who had never set foot on these shores before just got off the boat and came up to you and said, "I've made it to the United States, but will you please tell me how to get to America? I want to find the land of the free and home of the brave." We live in and by meanings that are not easy for us to tell others how to reach or find their way into.

IN THE RAGGED, RAW REAL

But we now descend from the realm of ideas into the arena of actuality, to meet Man in a particular condition, and consequently under limitations which do not originally derive from the mere conception of him, but from external circumstances and from a fortuitous exercise of his freedom. — *Friedrich Schiller*

Life must be taken as it is or left alone altogether. Try to distil it into biology or history and it turns into something else, for it is both of these and more. And just as the biology and history of life belong together, so too do the stuff and story of a human being. When we bring these two together, the language of life can begin to be heard.

A SELF AND STORY

What we make of life becomes our self and our story. Self and story emerge out of how we handle wants and needs, which leads us to both pleasure and pain. Our basic *needs* are few, less than ten in all: food, water, air, sleep, clothing/shelter, contact, withdrawal, elimination of waste, and — experiencing — through which they all come to life. If these needs are not met, in a very short time we can die.

Wants, however, are as limitless, varied, and colorful as all the creatures that have them; and new wants are invented each day and night. Unmet want produces anger, unmet need produces pain. But at the other end there is pleasure too — ecstatic joy, greater contentment — and everything else scattered in between.

First we are out to get what we need. Afterward, we reach further for what satisfies. We tell ourselves how nice it would be if we could do what we want. But we also can decide *not* to do what we want; both the doing and the not doing are chosen acts that come to make up part of our self and our story.

LIFE HAS ITS MOMENTS

Every now and then — in those little breaks in the bedrock of everything-as-usual, where movement is possible and there is space enough to turn around — the spontaneous occurs, something uncaused or unexpected emerges, and life is never again quite the same.*

Developments in neither biology nor history can be predicted, and this is true, as well, of our own biology and history. As the prominent biochemist and widely learned Erwin Chargaff so succinctly stated in his memoirs, "Life is the continual intervention of the inexplicable" (*Heraclitean Fire: Sketches from a Life before Nature,* New York: Warner Books, 1978). You never know when life is going to intrude, to pay you a visit or come for a stay, and set things stirring in you again . . . and again.

---

*I know of a man who said that each time he made one of the three major decisions of his life (to choose his career, to marry, to go in business for himself), he happened to be on an airplane. Trips are often one of the very kind of breaks mentioned here.

When such times come, at first it may not even seem like anything at all has happened — but it has, and all in a moment. Later, these occurrences may grow to become parts of our lives that are easy for us to see; so much so, in fact, that we have to exert ourselves a little to see much of the rest of it. What may help us to bring more of life's full sweep into view, is to become clearly acquainted with the fact that life not only has its moments, but it has its motions too. These motions are not to be taken as "stages" that all people undergo at some fairly fixed point in their life cycle; life is always too full of change, choice, and chance to ever be characterized in so fixed a fashion. These are general motions we humans go through, each of us at our own pace and in our own individual way.

GOING THROUGH THE MOTIONS
Experiencing

You see, now, that a man will never drop a link in his chain. He cannot. If he made up his mind to try, that project would itself be an unavoidable link — a thought bound to occur to him at that precise moment, and made certain by the first act of his babyhood. — Twain's *The Mysterious Stranger*

Experiencing is the most basic human act of all. It is the reach of life *in* the individual as well as the reaching for life *of* the individual that takes place soon after conception, when the human organism, at that precise time a veritable controlled explosion of cells in the womb, moves to make sense of all it meets. This primal act starts the life of the self, and it goes on each and every instant of a human being's life until death. It is the one act, more than any other, that forms our bodies and fashions our lives. The sense man makes, makes man.

Expanding

. . . the whole realm widens out again before me and around me — the air of life fills my lungs — the light of achievement flushes over all the place, and I believe, I see, I do.
—Henry James

Expanding is the movement of human life outward and upward in cellular growth, which is accentuated at birth but continues long afterward as the human organism extends into physical spacetime. This psychophysical forming keeps on as the tissues, organs, limbs, and muscles of the individual develop and his or her life unfolds. This basic burgeoning of the life-process makes its mark early as a prolonged undercurrent of motion and vitality.

Existing

I do not know who I am, what soul I have. . . . I feel beliefs which I do not hold. I am ravished by passions I repudiate.
— Fernando Pessoa

Existing is the action of positing oneself and one's life in the world, of being someone with definite needs and wants, and of moving to do something about it. This act exposes the individual to all the fascinations and frustrations that life holds, involving one "in the thick of it" right along with everyone else. This act makes the life of a child as worthy and real in its experiencing as that of any adult. Life is profound at any age.

Exploring

. . . one can mingle in the world with fresh perceptions only when one is young. The great thing is to be saturated *with something — that is, in one way or another, with life . . .*
— Henry James

Exploring is life moving on to take in and find out more. It is trust and care on the move, which arise respectively out of expanding and existing, participating in the act of *coming to know* more of self, others, and world. Once a human gets to its feet, the soft underbelly is exposed, and from then on its vulnerability is transported through the world as affectability — hence it is that we come to know more and more. Without exploring there is insufficient contact with the ongoingness of what is and what happens, and life stagnates in a sea of sameness.

Excursing

Where am I going? I don't know. When will I be there? I ain't certain. All I know is I am on my way.
> — Theme song from *Paint Your Wagon*

Excursing is setting out to find a life of one's own. It involves beginnings, breaks, and endings, in previous life-patterns. Leave-takings, whether accomplished geographically or symbolically, are of lasting importance because only those who leave home ever really find it. As exemplified in the biblical parable, it was the Prodigal Son's reach for what was rightfully his, his taking and using it all on his own, that enabled him to "come to himself." Clearly, there is no way to know if an individual is completely prepared for this step, because as much as anything it is the reaching itself that makes one ready. In general, if there is no reaching, then there is probably no readiness; for those who are ready, reach. This act births all genuine human responsibility.

Exerting

It is not my *work that interests me above all else; it is* work, *without a possessive pronoun, that must live . . .*
> — George Seferis

Exerting is the ambitious attempt to build the kind of life one wants in the world — to "find one's niche" or "make one's mark" in order to get on with the business of making one's life. It is the pouring of an individual's primary energies into those ways and means chosen to live life through, regardless of how they may be viewed or valued by the common crowd.

Our capacities and capabilities are far greater than most of us dare discern and develop, yet those can only be taken in hand through considerable toil and effort, and used by those willing to sweat fat and fluff off both body and brain, or turn them into muscle. This is the act, the motion of life, that measures individual capability and limit, thus providing a person with that personal frame of reference through which all the rest of life is primarily engaged.

Exceeding

I thought I was learning to live. I was only learning to die.
— A song from the Sixties

Exceeding is a life going beyond its earlier primary limits. If an earlier exerting did not determine these limits, then of course there can be no such clear and distinct going beyond them. This, by far, is the riskiest of all the motions of life, for it goes headlong into the most dangerous disruptions, upheavals, abrupt turnabouts, and reversals found in the experience of human beings.

It is a time when starting and stopping, pleasure and pain, laughing and crying, and living and dying no longer appear as opposites but rather as two different sides of the same thing. Life here is found to be bigger, badder, and better than it was ever known to be before — a reality still growing over against one that must be unflinchingly faced for what it is and isn't. Often there is a felt movement here from "there is something wrong with me if I don't fit the molds" to "there is something wrong with molds that don't fit me." It can be a time of the greatest follies, the flattest flops, and of the rarest findings. Context-puncture, which might occasionally occur in a few of the other motions here or there, *always* takes place here where many seldom seen realities are uncovered in self, others, the world — and in living and dying too. Those able to face death squarely are the ones who also begin to live life fully. They are those, of whom the world never has too many, who know there is ultimately no way out but through.

Expressing

Cursed be he who sees but does not speak. — Book of Jubilees

Expressing is living one's experiencing to the fullest and taking all the consequences of doing so. Few humans ever achieve much of this — for it is open only to those capable of crossing over through exceeding — and the genuineness of those who do is highly visible in their not having to hide either their successes or their failures. They know life is there more for the taking than it is for the asking — for who are we supposed to ask? If power is something people are waiting for others to give them, then it is probably something they are not yet ready to receive. If one is able to live with a No, then one is ready to ask for any Yes in the world.

This act of reaching forth to take life in one's own hands and use it is the most rudimentary expression of self-worth a human being is capable of; and it is the very opposite of selfishness (which always isolates), because this movement of life brings one into more contact with everything and everyone, not less.

Contrary to what is commonly taught, life is not undermined by those who reach forth for it, but by those who *don't*. Those who stand and seethe silently with anger at someone's choosing to live with, are usually more deeply angry at their own choosing to live without. No one around respects the reaching out for life more than another reacher. They know it for the life and death matter it actually is. Expressing is knowing where you stand and what to stand for, and doing it, and letting it show. It is that standing on one's ground which genuine *understanding* has always been. Without authentic expressing after exceeding, there is only a shrunken living. You never really help the being of another, or of the universe, by wiping out your own.

Extracting

We are a field of ripened grain . . . no longer green and not yet dried . . . We've reached the peak of the mountain and everything is clear up there on the peak: the way we came up, the way we'll go down. — Oriana Fallaci

Extracting separates the wheat from the chaff, keeps the essence of what one's life has matured into, and lets the rest fall by the wayside. It is a sifting and sorting whereby life's load is lightened. Letting go of what has long mattered is, in many ways, harder than deciding what matters in the first place. We become bonded to the things we have poured our life into. There are people who find this letting go so difficult that it is something they never do. Unable to end what has outlived its usefulness, such people wobble dangerously near to outliving their own — and a few do tumble on into that way of living.

Such a waning wobble is induced by seeing this necessary act only as a letting go, missing that instead it is essentially a separating out of and holding onto that which still lives, but which needs to be rooted in different soil if it is ever to bear fruit once more. This restructuring in life's later stages is usually accompanied by a restructuring of the body as well. These redoings inside and out combine in a most fundamental reforming, rearranging, rechanneling, and sometimes even relocating of a life's established patterns of work and play.

Extending

Every now and then I feel like I am twenty. And some days I feel about forty-five to fifty. Then, there are a few days when I actually do feel seventy-five. But most of the time I feel about thirty-two or thirty-three.

— A working actor at age seventy-five.

Extending is the keeping on with the work of nurturing what has been extracted. Without extracting there is no viable extending. A "niche" can actually be a rut that allows just enough motion to appear that its going somewhere. When a person has risen to the life-task of extracting, however, there is a vintage vitality left to pour into the channels one has then chosen to extend. This extending, in turn, provides the means for different points of contact and exchanges with life that may now lie in any quarter and run in all directions. One need not live the pace of youth, nor throb with its pulse, to bear still all the vigor of its spirit.

Extinguishing

. . . and he bowed his head and gave up his spirit.

— the Gospel of John

Extinguishing is the act of giving up experiencing, the reach of life and for life found in the individual. Though there may be no perceptible pause to deliberate, choosing enters into how we use what we have to become what we are. Choice is there in the reach of that sense we make at the very start, continues in that sense we make and live throughout it all, and choice is there too in how we come to let go of life at the very last.

WHO DO YOU THINK YOU ARE?

This venture of ours into making a life asked you first to use and then look at your own personal experiencing. If you entered fully into doing this, you should be able to reap the benefits of your earlier toils by bringing these two actions together now and making the most of them both to discover much more about the life you are making.

I. Pause for a Moment

A. Lay everything else aside and take a few minutes to think back over your life to a moment in which something happened that you have never forgotten.*

B. Let the memory of it fill your body as fully as possible so you can get the sense once more of what it was like from the inside out. Notice where in your body you seem to feel it the most, and pay attention to how you feel it.

C. Using your awareness to the utmost, glean any findings you can now that may shed light on how you embody and enact things that strike you.†

---

*A moment is not any set number of instants, but an *instance*, which the Oxford Universal Dictionary defines eloquently as "a case occurring." A moment might be less than a minute or longer than a month. It is simply something that happened to you; a whole of one kind or another.

†Since we so often focus on the external particulars of "what really happened," it may be worth noting here that the impact of such moments is due primarily to the personal meanings involved, which is to say that the striking thing one experiences takes place within the boundaries of one's own skin.

D. *Remember:* Since experience is the language of life, allowing yourself to have your experience fully is the first step towards hearing what some of the rest of your life has to say.

II. Experience the Sweep of Your Life: Where did you come from?

A. Go back to the beginning of Chapter 4 and thumb through its pages to read each one of the quotes or little epigraphs that start each section of that whole chapter. Take all of these in to "work the ground," breaking up the habitual posturings and plots of your mind in order to widen the access to your memory's store, and thus be able to better scan the immense range there in what you have experienced in life so far.

B. Mark those motions of life from page 52 through 58 with which you are acquainted firsthand, and note those which you have not yet experienced personally. What this should give you is a rough etching of the outline of your life so far. Do you see any signs of how you have or have not gone through any of these motions that seem characteristic of how your life moves?

C. Attempt to designate a major advantage and disadvantage that each of the motions of your life has left you with. Which of these do you value most; which do you value least?

D. Using these findings, ask yourself what time of life it is for you now. Which specific motions appear to be about to "catch up with you"? Which do you imagine you will enter into after the one or ones you find yourself in presently? (*Note:* By this time it must be obvious from the questions that individuals do not pass through these basic actions of human life in a strictly sequential fashion. Quite the contrary, they can build on each other so that a person is involved in more than one basic motion at a time. Also, with some individuals, actions ordinarily associated with later life may occur at a much earlier time.)

III. Locate your Realm of Experience: Where are you now?

A. Turn to the Locator on page 140 and use it to determine some of the formative personal preferences you have developed in your life. These can help you identify your strengths and shortcomings, which might prove useful in making long-range decisions in the future.

B. Use the Locator in conjunction with the overall realm of experience depicted on page 45. Try to clarify where your own experiencing is generally most active and least active.

C. Reading through the various motions of life mentioned in exercise II/B may have brought to mind some of your personal turning points. What would you say has been one of the major turning points in your life, and what effects has it had upon you?

D. What do you regard as the most important leave-taking you have made in life so far? Do you regard it as a failure, accomplishment, or something that was a mixture of both? (If you can find no major leave-taking, then explore your personal way of holding on to things.) What do you think is the most significant arriving or time of beginning in your life? (If you find it hard to choose from several, then how great a string of leavings are there?)

IV. Taking the Next Step:
Where are you going?

A. Take at least five minutes to write down on a piece of paper your answer to this question: What do those who know you best think you are good at?

B. Take five more minutes or so to write down the answers to these two questions:

    (1) What do you think you are best at?

    (2) What do you want to be best at?

(These may or may not come out the same.)

C. Complete the following sentences with as much specificity as you can muster:

    (1) What I would like more of in my life now is . . .

    (2) What I would like less of in my life now is . . .

(If a different response should cross your mind at a later time, then note such changes.)

D. Often an ounce of unclear *do* is worth a pound of perfectly clear "plan to." Try to pick a hunch you have had about some step you might take in your life next— and act on it. (*Warning:* it may not lead to all or anything that you expect, but it will hold more learnings about where your life is headed now than any book is able to — and, by no means will you find it boring.)

A VIEW FROM THE STERN

The first large ship I ever saw was the troop ship that took our company of Marines from Little Creek, Virginia, to the naval station at Roosevelt Roads, Puerto Rico, in the summer of 1954. We had been at sea for a few days; it was

hot, with little or no wind, and I climbed up on some crates at the stern to feel the ship's breeze and get a better view. Looking out at the cloudless sky and calm sea, I was amazed to see the traces of our wake still in the water trailing all the way back to the horizon. It was a watery path showing the way we had come, with every turn and mid-course maneuver there back as far as the eye could see.

Looking back now on our venture, it is plain to see that we too have traveled a long way, turning this way and that to move into and through some of the major moments and meanings of our own life. The next chapter makes up the longest stretch in our voyage, and it will bring us into those waters near our final destination.

· 6 ·

SEEING THE SOUL

> To attain any assured knowledge about the soul is one
> of the most difficult things in the world.   —*Aristotle*

> The ones we love the most are not those who give us
> something we did not have before, but those who show
> us the richness of what we already possess.   —*Pascal*

The longest leg of our voyage has begun. On it we will
need experience, awareness, everything we have worked
on so far — all that and more. For what we are going to
try to do now is catch a glimpse of your *soul*.

WHY BRING THAT UP?

> *My language is the universal whore whom I have to make
> into a virgin.*   — Karl Kraus

"Soul" is an ancient word. It is in the Bible. Plato used it.
Aristotle used it even more. And so have countless others
all over the world for thousands of years. About a hundred
years ago, however, the word "soul" started to fall out of
use in the Western World.* Since our times and language

---

*This loss is well documented in Western literature and art. Quite un-
derstandably, it was when we were losing the word that the "science of
the soul," psychology, began to be established. A special section refer-
ring to this development will be found in the back of the book in the
section marked For Those Who Want To Read More, which contains
selections treating the subject of the soul.

are part of the givens of our background, this dropping out of the word has had effects upon us from which we cannot escape.

For years, "soul" meant some phantasm that was as insubstantial and unattached as the word for it was. A poet or songwriter could use it all right, but it certainly did not stand for anything that was "really real." After I had completed my schooling and become pleasantly situated in my new career, I started feeling the vaguest sense of something missing. At first it was so slight that it passed unnoticed except at the quietest times. Then as it grew I thought I needed to look for — for what? I didn't know. At that time, getting away from everything or everyone for a while and walking, walking, walking was the only thing that seemed to suggest I was "getting somewhere" with it; though the relief this brought was perhaps little more than tiring myself out so I could not feel the nagging nudge anymore. Later on I saw that was where my life took a turn and started moving in a different direction. This motion, which eventually emerged as the act of exceeding, became ever more pronounced, and though for the life of me I would not then have been able to express what it meant, I nevertheless knew it was significant, and that something very real was there. I had felt the first inkling of my soul, and what I learned later was that this is what the ancients had been talking about all along. And what is the soul? Just this: *The soul is the quality of your life that persists across time.** It is the specific uniqueness that quickens your own life-process.

----

*Some habits of thought in our background tempt us to believe, as I once did, that only physical things are "really there." But if this were so, we would have to declare that fire, which is pure process, does not exist; or, that there is no such thing as a reflection, and what one sees when peering over the edge of a spring in the forest is nothing at all.

FOR ALL TO SEE

What do we see when we look at someone? Do we see the "real person" or just a kind of husk or shell, the outward and visible sign of an inward and invisible "self"? Do we see all there is to see, the full human being — or can we only see the human and not the being?*

It is possible to scrutinize every particle of a human being with an electron microscope, and yet not know who or what they are at all. You still would not know if they vote Democrat or Republican, or ever bother to go to the polls; if they like classical music, jazz, country and western, hard rock, disco, the new wave, or don't like music at all. You could not tell if they were political activists, religious mystics, health enthusiasts, financial wizards, or research scientists; whether they were artistically creative, mechanically inclined, good at building things, had a "green thumb," "a head for figures," "a place for everything and everything in its place," or were usually "a day late and a dollar short,"

---

*The different views on this issue are so established that they have their own classic names. Some say, "There is no difference between the two because finally all is One" (mysticism); "There is essence *and* existence" (idealism or essentialism), or "essence *in* existence" (scientism or realism), or "essence *as* existence" (existentialism); while others say, "It is all in how you look at it" (phenomenalism), "What is there is all that matters" (materialism), "What I don't know is not so" (solipsism), "I know the answer" (gnosticism), "I don't know the answer and no one else does either" (skepticism), "I am not sure what I know and don't know" (agnosticism), "All I know is what I know, and that is all anyone else can know either" (relativism), and "Who cares, anyway?" (cynicism). Which view, or mixture of them, comes closest to your own?

or "one step ahead of the sheriff." Nor would you know whether they were neat, sloppy, warm or cold; whether they "fly off the handle," or whether they "had the patience of Job," "give it their all" or "just get by." Nor would you have a reason to guess if they looked upon life as something romantic, tragic, ironic, or comic, or know what they have ever left or put behind them, when and where they ever experienced love, or personally came across death and dying, or how they did all of these things physically; nor would you know whether they sneeze or stifle it, or breathe from their chest, belly, or diaphragm, dream in color or seldom dream at all, have a good memory or a bad one, are invigorated more by the beach or by the mountains, are a "day person" or a "night person," or sleep all curled up or all stretched out. Without knowing such things as these, and many others like them, we have no sense at all of who the person is that stands before us.

COMING INTO VIEW

Only when things such as those just mentioned come into view can we start to see the soul. Yet mention the word "soul," and right away people start looking for something with wings, when for all humans something with feet will actually suit just fine. The human soul is not so light that one must look for it in the air, or so heavy that we must search out the depths, nor even so abstract that we have to "go into the mind" (whatever that means, exactly) in order to find it. It will be found there in your own life, in what and how you are living right now — and you already know where and what that is because we have been dealing with it from the moment you first opened this book. It is alive and shows itself in everything you experience, enact, and embody. Anything done to the body is done to the soul. Whoever would deal with your soul must therefore deal with your body.* So your soul is always there, and always as big as your whole life. That is why the soul can only be seen in a life, and there, only in its way of living that lasts across time.

What more can we say of the soul? Only that we must set out to explore it before we sit down to explain it. And how can we manage to accomplish this? By selecting the lives of actual human beings and looking into them for signs of how the soul abides there throughout.

MODES OF HUMAN BECOMING

It is more difficult to describe one actor than to write a whole philosophy of art, and more difficult to describe one of his performances than to describe the actor. — Soren Kierkegaard

On this last and longest stretch of our voyage, we must ready ourselves to make sightings of the soul. This can only be done by scanning the whole of a life, taking cognizance of its specific vitality and looking for its ways of living that continue across time. Though this is not easy, it is possible, and what it can teach us about human life makes it well worth the effort.

Bespeaking: the Artistic Experience of Life

Basically, I'm really just a hoofer. — James Cagney

The TV picture was on, but the volume was off. An awards banquet, it looked like, with celebrities in tuxedos

---

*Entrust no one with your soul, least of all a guide or "spiritual director" who does not also show an understanding of and great respect for your body. Those who would try to "guide your spirit" without hearing your body speak eloquently and deeply of your life, for all their good intentions, only tend to pollute the spirit and imprison the soul. That is why what we are after is for you to hear, and learn to speak, the language of your own life.

and long evening gowns. Everything was glitter, glisten, and shine — strictly Show Biz at its fancy usual. I was packing to catch an owly-bird flight and had no time to get distracted by that. Starting to flick off the set, I noticed George C. Scott flash onto the screen. But he never went to such banquets, and would let it be known that if he was given an award he would not receive it. Why was he there? I upped the volume just as he was ending his speech, which ran something like:

> . . . and so I'll conclude with the fitting words I read once in a biography of Robert E. Lee. "He was what he seemed: a simple man; noble, religious." That, to me, is James Cagney.

James Cagney? That was quite a while back. All of those gangster, tough-guy, rat-a-tat roles like Cody Jarrett, who goes crazy at the end in *White Heat* when he hears his mother died, so he blows himself up by shooting holes in the flaming gas tank he was standing on. Was he still around? The TV camera answered affirmatively, zooming in for a close-up of Cagney's face. And there it was, that still recognizable, slightly pugnacious mug, topped now by a thick crop of snowwhite hair. He sat there without a ripple of expression.

As the show went on, one famous star after another came forth to pay tribute ("Oh *her;* yeah, she was in . . . ; and *that* guy; didn't he play in . . . "). The remarks were both written and spontaneous, silly and sentimental, but regardless of the wrappings, what the package held was honest-to-God respect. And each time the camera zoomed in on that leonine head, hoping to catch some show of feeling — an emotional nod, maybe, or a memory-filled smile — there was that strangely blank face ("They wouldn't have invited him, would they, if senescence . . . aw, he's not *that* old; but still, he is awfully quiet"). His expression had the same general effect as an empty theatre marquee. The director and the switchman in the control booth must have been tearing their hair.

At last, they showed some of Cagney's song and dance numbers as George M. Cohan in *Yankee Doodle Dandy*. As the houselights came back up and the audience was still reverberating with such tunes as "Give My Regards to Broadway," and others, Cagney began making his way down the main aisle toward the front. Just then the crowd, finding a channel for its brimming enthusiasm, burst into a rhythmic clapping to the beat of "I'm A Yankee Doodle Dandy," to which the honored guest, showing the first recognizable signs of his old self on camera that evening, started a slight bouncing to the beat as he continued down the aisle, up the stairs, and across the stage to the speaker's stand. There he stopped, turned, and blurted somewhat breathlessly into the mike, "I'm a wreck." And everybody laughed and settled back into their seats. He then went on to say that after he'd been told about the plans for the evening, he asked his friend A. C. Lyles, "But what will the people expect of me? It's not the kind of thing I do everyday." To which Lyles had replied, "All you have to do is . . . uhm . . . uhh . . . uhm." And Cagney had asked, "What's that?" And Lyles gave the same uhms and uhhs again. "So . . . " Cagney continued, "with the inflection appropriate to the occasion, I say to you here, one and all, uhm, uhh, uhm, uhh." Everyone howled.

In an instant Cagney had punctured the pretention of a setting where everyone is "on" and playing roles, thus creating a little clearing — and he did it as effortlessly and naturally as that splendid gesture he improvised on the spot in *The Oklahoma Kid*, when he reached up to "feel the air." Having made that clearing, he now stepped into it, and then James Cagney, that experienced old hand, reached out to take the "more" provided by the occasion, and there shaped and molded it into a moment that unleashed his own vitality and evoked that of others. He did it by speaking about art:

> Art. Now, I'm a little bit hipped on the thing myself and have been for a long time. William Ernest Hocking said, "Art is life — plus caprice." But it also brings to mind a work written by John Masefield, the English poet laureate. He wrote it with a pen dipped in a bit of vitriol. I'm going to read it to you now.

> What is the hardest task of art?
> To clear the ground and make a start
> 'Midst wooden head and iron heart;
> To sing the stopp'd adder's ear
> To fill the tale with none to hear,
> And paint what none else reckon dear;
> To dance or carve or build or strive
> Among the dead or half alive
> Whom greeds impel and terrors drive.
> Now you, my English dancers, you
> Began our English joy anew
> In sand with neither rain nor dew,
> Dance was despised and held in shame
> Almost something not to name
> But that lovely flower came.
> Oh, may you prosper till the race
> Is all one rapture at your grace,
> And England Beauty's dwelling place.
> Then you'll know what Shakespeare knew
> That when the millions want the few
> They can make heaven here — and do.

Even as he spoke, he created what he was reading about — before the audience's very eyes. James Cagney knew what he was doing; so well, in fact, that he didn't have to think about it while he did it. He had done it so many, many times before that for him it had long since become a means of heightened presence. Richard Southern, another man who understands this underlying act of the artist, penned this vivid description of it:

> Whenever an individual addresses a group ... then he is facing a strength that is capable of overpowering his own ... This very strength is the power which the individual can, provided he has the personality and skill, take to his advantage ... That is why behind all the essentials of technique which should be in his equipment as regard voice, gesture, costume and the rest, there lies one deeper essential still, the essential of feeling that audience-reaction and of responding to that feeling, but of also being able to engage it to convey to the public whatever happens to be the subject of his address to them ... It is a twofold opportunity; the opportunity to *take* the power of a gathering to oneself and to dominate; this is a proud and selfish motive, and it is very characteristic of a player to show himself off. Or the opportunity to *give*, to seize the power of a gathering to convey to them ... what? A vestige of the godhead. This, curiously, is a very humble motive; and even more curiously it is equally characteristic of the player ... to give of himself without return.
>
> Thus we have the roots of the player's two major characteristics: his selfishness and his generosity. These will affect the theatre forever.
>
> In just the same way, since so many of these things are concerned with fighting against death, and with birth and resurrection, so the player will unleash another characteristic, that of his or her vitality as a man or woman. (R. Southern, *The Seven Ages of the Theater*, New York: Hill & Wang, 1963, pp. 24–27)

Cagney shows this understanding too by putting this original verse at the very beginning of his own autobiography: "Each man starts with his very first breath, To devise shrewd means for outwitting death." This delightful autobiography, modest yet masterful,* shows a man given to the artistic experience of life. There is his continually being struck to the quick by beauty, as in a moment when he burst into tears at seeing a ballerina alight from her ascent; his being deeply stirred at the sight of total effort in both foot races and horse races; his never having to "psych up" to play a scene — for he never got himself into the phony position of believing he had to *be* the part he was playing (therefore, he would have no difficulty accessing and using what he had and who he was); his fifty-year ongoing effort to preserve the natural beauty of the land; his distaste for directing other actors ("I have no interest in telling other people their business"); and his dislike of bad directors — all of which shows his overwhelming respect for the natural and his unceasing resistance to whatever pollutes it; his exquisite sense of timing, found in his pacing of a dialog or scene, and in his ability to pinpoint the moment, knowing when it was over and time for the curtain (which, it seems, even told him during the filming of *One, Two, Three* that his career in pictures had come to its natural end: "I knew at that moment that I would never bother about acting anymore."); his taking up painting at age sixty and staying engrossed in it; his poetry; and, throughout, his abiding involvement in simple wonder, one which continues to grow; and . . . more.

James Cagney is a man who knows who he is, what he is — and lives it. That is why in his films so much vitality

---

*Modest in magnitude because it is a third the size of most film star autobiographies, and modest in manner as Cagney, despite his "unmistakable touch of the gutter," is known to be (many actors and artists handle their person much like they do their creative efforts: keeping them under wraps or behind the curtain until that time — and it doesn't always come — when they are rightly formed); masterful, because he wrote it himself and so his personal quality shows through.

comes through. And it was for *that,* and for the spark such genuineness ignites in others, that Cagney was being honored.

James Cagney bespeaks the artistic experience of life in a human soul that is ever reaching out to grasp the "more" that is there, and to strive to render it into expressive form.* To bespeak means to "be the outward expression of" (Oxford English Dictionary). Bespeaking means fashioning one's "more" into an artistic act and experience of life. He once wrote some words about a friend's poem. They fittingly point to the soul of the actor, the artist — and, therefore, the very life of James Cagney, the man:

> From first to last, it bespeaks life involvement and that wonderful gift that comes free to us all if we will only take it — and with which life is enriched beyond all description — wonder.

Believing: the Religious Experience of Life

My purpose in writing was not beauty, it was deliverance. — Nikos Kazantzakis

Anyone who is unwilling to grapple with spirit had better leave Nikos Kazantzakis alone — for spirit emptied his life and fills his works. And those to whom spirit is a mere term or a hollow concept will not be able to understand either the man or his works. But if they should want to try, then let them pick up something — anything — this Cretan ever wrote. As they hold it in their hands, beginning to take in his words through their eyes, let them see what happens

---

*Shakespeare, of course, pointed to this configurative act in the work of the poet: "As imagination bodies forth the forms of things unknown, the poet's pen turns them to shape, and gives to airy nothing, a local habitation and a name."

inside them when, like someone who is not expecting a visitor and suddenly hears his door open and someone enter, his own soul rushes out to see who it is. When all at once some phrase, sentence, or passage kindles recognition in his soul, then let him wonder at the quiver of life within him — at what it is and where it comes from.

When Kazantzakis was born, the old midwife brought him close to the light and examined him with great care. Then, as if reading some mystic sign on him, she lifted him high up and said, "Mark my words: One day this child will become a bishop." Later, when he learned of this prophecy, Kazantzakis believed it because it matched his most secret yearnings. So he set out to do only that which he thought a bishop might do, until the day he came to see what bishops really did, and changed his mind. "Thenceforth, in order to deserve the sainthood I so craved, I wished to avoid all things that bishops do." And he did. Throughout his life he would reject anything and everything not big enough to be lived — and the power of life within him would batter and smash against those things. And how would he know what was big enough to allow spirit the breathing room it must have or die? There was really only one way — risky, but sure; and he set out doing it about as soon as he learned to walk.

> One day in school we read in our primer that a child fell down a well and found himself in a fabulous city with gilded churches, flowering orchards, and shops full of cakes ... My mind caught fire. Running home, I tossed my satchel in the yard and threw myself upon the brim of the well so that I could fall inside and enter the fabulous city. My mother ... uttered a cry, ran, and seized me by the smock just as I was kicking the ground in order to hurl myself headforemost into the well.

All of his life, when there was no one to protect or stop him, Kazantzakis would hurl himself into the deepest wells of humankind; Art, Religion, Politics, Philosophy . . . to find out where it led, or drown. He did not calculate shrewdly or bargain like Faust, holding out until the terms were right; but he simply handed over his whole existence — body, mind, soul, and spirit — to trying the way of those who have pointed the way for humankind, to see if their paths did indeed lead to life: Homer, Moses, St. Theresa, Buddha, Dante, Christ, Nietzsche, Muhammed, Genghis Khan, Shakespeare, Don Quixote, Lenin, El Greco, and others. Kazantzakis struggled in his spirit to meet theirs with no holds barred. Each encounter left a mark on his soul, giving to him and taking from him something, so that he would never be quite the same again.

Few humans treading this earth ever risk the total abandonment of a true pilgrimage, let alone undergo the danger and disintegration of a journey so vast in scope as that undertaken by Kazantzakis. Few who set out on such a journey persist to the end, and of these, only a handful produce anything that transcends their personal search and passes on something that others can use to advance further still. Had he been a man of thought or a man of action, he might have chosen to walk either path to distinction — as thousands of other genuinely outstanding people have done. But both strivings were in him, as they are to a degree in everyone, and they turned up early in his life, when he was still a schoolboy. His response hinted even then that he was one who would choose to live them both.

> So audacious did my mind become, that one day I made the harum-scarum decision that next to every word in the French dictionary I would write the Greek equivalent. This labor took me months . . . and when I finally finished . . . I took it and proudly showed it to Père Laurent, the school's director, a learned Catholic priest. "What you have done, my young Cretan, shows that one day you will become an important man. You are fortun-

ate in having found your road while so young. Scholarship — that is your road. God bless you."

Filled with pride, I ran as well to the assistant director,
Père Lelièvre, a well-fed, fun-loving monk with playful
eyes. "Shame on you!" he screamed. "Are you a boy or
a doddering old graybeard? Out of my sight! Take it
from me that if you follow this road, you'll never amount
to anything — never! You'll become some miserable
round-shouldered little teacher with spectacles. If you're
really a Cretan, burn this damnable dictionary and bring
me the ashes. Then I'll give you my blessing. Think it
over and act. Away with you."

I went away completely confused. Who was right, what
was I to do? Which of the two roads was correct? This
question tortured me for years, and when I finally discovered which road was the correct one, my hair had
turned gray.

This happened when Kazantzakis was a boy; holding to
both strivings, he wandered the world and became a man.
When one striving was pursued, content in being tended
to and followed, discontent and, at times, disease, would
drive the other into a resounding lament that built into a
piercing temple-cracking cry that would make him turn
and follow it.

Thought and *action* taunted him like two seductive sirens.
Untied to any mast, he took the cotton from his ears, and
then followed, living the torment of conflicting lures and
screams — until he found, amidst the swell of rage and
clamor, the still small voice of his own soul. At times the
tension nearly tore his life apart. To ease this, most people
would let one of these mighty strivings go, and lob it out
of significant awareness, holding from then on with both
hands firmly to the other. Kazantzakis didn't. Like a man
trying to tame two steeds, each lunging in a different direction, Kazantzakis held onto both. This guaranteed
that his life would become a pilgrimage, for that is what a

true pilgrimage is: a journey combining thought with action, a living of both. He undertook the pilgrimage, persisted in it to the very end, and in so doing created the unfolding journey of his life.

And journey is what he did, starting with *Greece* — "the filter which, with great struggle, refines brute into man, eastern servitude into liberty, barbaric intoxication into sober rationality" — where, "The spirit has trodden upon the stones . . . for many, many years; no matter where you go, you discover its divine traces"; *Italy and Assisi* — where "For the entire extent of this honeymoon with my soul I felt, to a greater degree then ever again in my life, that body, mind, and soul are fashioned of the same clay. Only when a person ages or falls into the grips of illness or misfortune do they separate and oppose one another"; *Mount Athos* — " . . . since I myself could not become either a saint or a hero, I was attempting by means of writing to find some consolation for my incapacity" — where he and his poet friend, thinking they were a team of oxen, yoked together and, plowing the earth, "plowed the air" in youth's needful Quixotic assault upon life; *Jerusalem* — "the sun-baked land where once upon a time a flame had bounded out of a poor cottage in Nazareth, a flame which burned and renewed man's heart" — the place on the voyage to which, "The ship's hold seemed like a new catacomb in which slaves had assembled once more — today's slaves — to conspire to blow the world up all over again . . . High up in first class, the carefree faithless talked politics . . . while here below, deep down in the hold, we were carrying as a terrifying gift the seed of a new, dangerous, and as yet unformed cosmogony"; *The Desert and Sinai* — where an old monk, about to die, entrusts him with the fruit of the monk's apprenticeship in life to flesh and spirit . . . "You are rendering up the flame of your entire life. Will I be able to carry it still further and turn it into light?"; *Crete* — where his father, unsatisfied with his only and wandering son, said, bidding him farewell at the waterfront, "I think you're like your grandfather . . . I don't mean your mother's father, but mine, the pirate. But he rammed ships . . . What ships are you ramming?"; *Paris* — where he studied under the philosopher Bergson, and dove into that martyr to truth, Nietzsche; *Vienna* — where he discovered Buddha, and was also afflicted by a tormenting illness that swelled his face so that his eyes shut almost completely, which the renowned Freudian, Wilhelm Stekel, diagnosed as "ascetic's disease," common in the Middle Ages but almost unheard of in modern times . . . "because what body today, obeys its soul?" . . . and which cleared, as Stekel said it would, as soon as Kazantzakis left behind both Vienna and the woman he had met there; *Berlin* — where his Buddhism was punctured by the great misery of human suffering, hunger, oppression . . . shaming him into a responsibility which linked him from then on with all the rest of humankind — and where he first met Albert Schweitzer; *Russia* — Lenin, Marx, and the Slavic soul and land where the awesome bloody experiment was taking place . . . "Miracle butts against reality, makes a hole, and enters" *The Caucasus* — where he moved completely into action in taking, as he was asked to, the directorship of Greece's Ministry of Social Welfare, in order to rescue 100,000 Greeks endangered by the Bolsheviks on the north and the Kurds on the south . . . "The moment was ripe to test whether action, by slicing its sword through the insoluble knots of speculation, was alone capable of giving an answer"; *Crete* — returning home . . . "Having just returned from Russia, I too wished to make this microscopic attempt to emerge from my ivory tower and work with human beings." And then . . . "as if fate was in a mood to play games" . . . he met Giorghos Zorba . . . "this dancer and warrior, the broadest soul, surest body, freest cry I ever knew in my life." (The account of this pilgrimage, filled with rare and truly magnificent discoveries, is laid out before the reader in Kazantzakis' *Report to Greco;* New York: Bantam, 1966.)

Then he stopped to catch his breath from the grueling pace of the spiritual marathon he had been on for forty years. The air he now breathed in blew like wind across a field of grain, and it shook loose the seed of his soul, which fell to the ground within him, took root, and began to sprout. For years he had had a definite aim.

> My aim is not Art for Art's sake, but to find and express a new sense of life . . . In the process of writing I feel increasingly relieved. And yet I know that this is by no means enough. To attain my aim, I must make a leap. As soon as this leap is accomplished (which can only be an example of life and not one of Art and writing), I shall find the expression of my soul . . .

Now that aim took shape. As he began to find his soul, a living form emerged: Zorba, whom he then used to re-fashion an ancient form into something big enough to pour his forty years of thought and action into, and which was: " . . . Odysseus; he was the mold I was carving out so that the man of the future might flow in." In this act and work, his "Obra," a remarkable metamorphosis occurred: what he was struggling to create now began to actualize within himself. In the fourteen years he was metamorphosing Odysseus from the happenings of the past, his own substance was transubstantiating into the stuff of the future. Sitting down to write out of the odyssey he had lived, he commenced to live the odyssey of which he wrote — and arose a different man.

> If he had allotted fourteen years to model his Odysseus, the "future man," Odysseus in his turn had allotted fourteen years to model the future Kazantzakis. And when the umbilical cord was snapped, there were two men — mature, serene, walking hand in hand along the

rim of the abyss. The osmosis of life and death took place gently, "admirably," open-eyed. (Helen Kazantzakis, *Nikos Kazantzakis*, New York: Simon and Schuster: 1968, p. 384.)

This, by far, was the most critical period of Kazantzakis' life. During this time he was sure he was wasting his life, was thunderstruck in totally different ways by his mother's death, and then his father's, lost some of his closest friends, had the deepest doubts about his writing, experienced a series of severe setbacks with publishers, and underwent extreme personal and financial hardship. Yet at the same time, he focused his life's elusive purpose in a single sentence, ("It is not human beings that interest me, but the flame that consumes human beings." Ibid, p. 214.), found his most natural style, heard the cry of the future, entered fully into his Age, wrote *The Odyssey*, and then launched forth, unencumbered and renewed, into the future. He had made it through life's straits. To be sure, there in the narrows much had washed overboard and tumbled into the rough dark waters of the deep. But like the little skiff he saw in a dream, his heart kept scudding along in the narrow crack left between the menacing sky and pitch-black raging sea, billowing full-sail toward the open waters.

Kazantzakis had found vitality in a form he thought he was unsuited for and not able to handle: the novel. A torrent of novels then rushed forth. Still true to his aim, his primary thrust in this venture of body, mind, and soul was not artistic but religious — genuinely religious. As Martin Buber defined it: "The realer religion is, so much the more it means its own overcoming. It wills to cease to be the special domain 'Religion' and wills to become life" (*The Eclipse of God*, New York: Harper & Row, 1952). Instead of using life's power to create expressive forms, he came at it the other way around, seeking to find expressive forms that the power of life might use. While art is a movement of life into form, religion is a movement of form into life. In the first, spirit becomes matter, and in the second, matter becomes spirit. He was after a way to extend spirit, to stretch it in order that life could have the breathing room in which to form him and all humankind anew, thereby lifting man higher and planting him with both feet on the new ground of the age just dawning.

> I used to believe that there must be a great difference between vital literary work and action. A genuine novelist can live only in his own time, and by living this reality he acquires consciousness of his own responsibility and assumes the duty of helping his fellowmen to envisage and solve, as far as possible, the crucial problems of his era. If he acquires consciousness of his mission, the novelist endeavors to compel the reality that is flowing formlessly to take on the form he regards as most worthy of man . . . .

As Kazantzakis labored in the vineyard of this unfamiliar genre, thought and action joined and produced offspring. Each novel was a furthering step in his pain-filled yet joyous ascent, and meant another trip to the rim of the abyss, to look into it unflinchingly and leap, so that he would have to sprout wings to keep from perishing. Each new novel was thus a stretching of his outermost boundaries, a making of still more of his soul into spirit; so each one, a little odyssey in itself, drained more of his life from him. Helen could plainly see the exhaustion hollowing out the face of her companion as he continued his chosen path:

> I've struggled, that's true, throughout my life. And I'm still struggling to keep my soul from dying. I know how the mortal becomes immortal. And this is precisely the great torment of my life. For it is not enough that you know. You must also become . . .

Finally, on October 26, 1967, sick with fever, while

Helen was at his side he made his final leap into the abyss and rendered the last bit of his life into spirit.

> Confronting death as he had lived, he had just given up his soul. "Like a king who had taken part in the festivity, then risen, opened the door and, without turning back, crossed the threshold.

"I had been struggling for a lifetime to stretch my mind until it creaked at the breaking point in order to bring forth a great idea able to give a new meaning to life, a new meaning to death, and comfort to men."

What he had been struggling to do in his lifetime, Nikos Kazantzakis achieved. Faith is that upon which one is willing to act. To *believe* is to be and live more and more in the light of the ultimate, so that one's life becomes filled with it. Believing means fashioning one's "more" into a religious act and experience of life. For Kazantzakis, the élan of life came through this ardent desire. "We call 'nonexistent' whatever we have not desired with sufficient strength." Thus his life was an enactment of adoration, and it is the efficacy of his ever-transcending act that pours into the lives of thousands of others as spirit. Early in his life he had wanted to found a new religion. He failed in that, yet succeeded in doing much more. Because far greater than that which only brings in something new, is something strong enough to make even something old new again. The tremendous might of his spirit broke the crust into which much religion had hardened for centuries, exposing again the good bread underneath, so it could be eaten and nourish to life the hungry souls of the world once more. And the power of his life, with its far-reaching effects, are visible in what happened at his funeral on the island of Crete, which both the church and the state sought, unsuccessfully, to suppress.

> They were here from every village and city . . . 50,000 of them, to pay final homage to the writer who had

wandered the earth and always returned home to squeeze a clod of Cretan soil in his palm and draw strength from it . . .

Everything went as planned — the tributes, the placing of flowers — until it came time to lower the coffin into the grave. Then a giant of a man, a veritable Zorba, stepped out of the crowd . . . Captain Mamousakas . . . his mustache was large, sweeping, ferocious . . . "Such a man as this," he rumbled, "must be put into his grave by heroes." So saying, he picked up the head of the coffin by himself. His three friends took hold of the other end. Together they lowered Nikos Kazantzakis into his personal abyss. (Frank Riley, "A Cross In Heraklion,"*Saturday Review,* October 14,1967,pp. 47-48.)

His life, long since turned to spirit, was stirring souls here and elsewhere in the world. The same spirit is there in the flame his work kindles in souls today.

Beholding: the Philosophic Experience of Life

There is no truth without the way to truth. — Paul Tillich

Words — to a few they matter as much, but to none do they matter more than they do to . . . a philosopher. There are not very many of these in our midst. There never have been and are never likely to be. Several people teach philosophy — read, think, lecture, and maybe even write about it, but that is not enough to make anyone a philosopher.

That happens only when someone, sauntering through life, stumbles one day upon the astonishing fact that his picture of the world is just that: *his picture* and nothing more. He then feels what he had always stood on start to crumble and give way beneath him — and right there he experiences that hiatus, that crack or gap, in which philosophy is born.

Discovering this gap does not make one a philosopher either, though it does create the possiblility for it. Only if the individual turns to face the uncertainty, to take it in and digest it, so that it is reconstituted into a question that sends him out into the world to seek its answer — only *then* does he become a philosopher. From that time on he will pay the closest attention to words so he can phrase his questions and share his answers. Others without this experience are likely to look upon such a person as much too preoccupied with this or that, and far too picky about his points. If such an individual should go on to become a good philosopher, he or she will convey, as much by manner as message, the reason for the carefulness: namely, the outcome of these questions and answers will make a difference in how they live their lives. That is why words matter so much to such persons. Moreover, if, as they make use of them, they struggle hard to keep them on to what matters to them most — having the courage to show that forth, whatever it may bring or lead to — then their words will have an unusual genuineness that will resonate in other human beings with issues genuinely their own. A philosopher good enough to do all this becomes great. Paul Tillich stumbled upon the philosophic gap early in life, took in the experience of it, and became a philosopher — a good one, and a great human being.

Shortly before he died in 1965, Tillich was at the University of California in Berkeley for a short unpublicized stay. By little more than word of mouth, seven thousand people showed up to hear him speak. The turnout is no surprise to those who had heard him before. They had seen the same thing for themselves. That slow, ponderous, thickly accented voice, positioning each thought as carefully as the medieval stonemasons picked and patted into place each stone to construct the Gothic cathedrals of Europe. Tillich lectured without gesture or fanfare, yet to hear him was gripping; because his presence was that of one who himself was grasped by something.

> When I was of the age to receive confirmation . . . I was told to choose a passage from the Bible as the expression of my personal approach to the biblical message . . . When I chose the words "Come unto me all ye that labor and are heavy laden," I was asked . . . why I had chosen that particular passage . . . I could not answer at that time; I felt a little embarrassed, but basically right, indeed: every child is right in responding immediately to those words . . . They are simple; they grasp the heart . . . disturbing the mind of the wise . . . Returning for the first time in my life to the passage of my early choice, I feel just as grasped by it as at that time . . .*(P. Tillich, *Perspectives on 19th and 20th Century Protestant Theology*, New York:Harper & Row, 1967)

Paul Tillich molded his natural vitality as a human being into thought. It became his way of life as thinking became his most characteristic activity. But thought is much like an underground river that widens and deepens as it winds its way without being seen — which is why this unhurryable gift can pass undetected even by those who have been given it — until it eventually breaks through the surface and gushes out in an unstemmable flow of worded deliberations.

On the surface, the path of his life showed nothing uncommon as he was reared in the German town of Schönfliess, and later boarded away in Königsberg for two years to attend the humanistic Gymnasium there. In 1900, at age fourteen, his family moved to Berlin, where he graduated from school, went on to pursue theological studies, acquired both his Doctor of Philosophy and Licentiate of

---

*It was this same quality of being grasped that led Henry Sloan Coffin to comment to Rollo May, upon hearing Tillich's first lectures in this country, "I don't understand what he says, but when I look at his face I believe" (R. May, *Paulus*, New York: Harper & Row, 1973).

Theology, and was ordained in the Evangelical Lutheran Church. After World War I, in which he served as a chaplain, he was finally able to launch his academic career at thirty-three years of age by becoming a teacher at the University of Berlin in 1919.

It was beneath the surface, and only with time, that the great flow of his thought developed. It started in his childhood as the trickle of a spring in Schönfliess, a setting of the past in which he had early and lasting "experiences of the holy" amidst its medieval city-walls and Gothic church. As a brook it then babbled its way along through the young Paulus's years of instruction, with classical antiquity stretching along its one bank and Christian tradition along the other, before turning into the tumbling stream of a romanticist involvement in all nature, heightened by annual family visits to the North Sea. This stream grew into a young river cascading into the virile fascinations and cultural enticements of such a worldly sprawl as Berlin, with the onrushing waters gathering unto themselves the impact and residue of his mother's death when Tillich was seventeen. The river widened quickly as it spilled out onto the broad terrain of a world at war, of politico-economic clashes in postwar revolution, and of collapsing intellectual and religious beliefs and ideas. In full view for the first time, the depth and power of this river of thought attracted the first real attention to itself in Berlin, continued onto traverse a somewhat obscure bend through the city of Marburg, coming fully into its own at Dresden, there settling into the channel and current that would carry it to its final destination.

Paul Tillich did not think as he did because of what he lived, but lived as he did because of how he thought. He did not try to mold the "more" into expressive form, as art does, nor, like religion, to use it to forge some new tunnel or pathway to life; instead, he employed it to *discern* form in life and existence. So, he commenced to experience life philosophically.

> That means participating in the form of things. Read-able things have a form. The substance, the dynamics, you cannot read; they are dark; they are the drives. Reading, which is here meant metaphorically, is only possible where there is form. The word "understanding" has a similar metaphorical meaning. Standing under or reading between have the same meaning. They refer to a position in which we are in the reality itself and are able to become aware of its particular form. (P. Tillich, *19th & 20th Century Protestant Theology,* p. 196.)

Whenever he wrote or spoke about life, in general or his own, he portrayed it as a dance of ideas. For him, ideas were like living things that came and went, lived and died, and either led a person toward more life or away from it — though he usually found them to be "ambiguous," a mix-ture of both. Nevertheless, he did not come at ideas the way a scholar, a *Gelehrte,* attempts to "master" them by ex-hausting awareness alone. He was after something more: he wanted to actually connect with the life and power of an idea. Unwilling to settle for its husk, he wanted its heart. Instead of stopping after grasping the form of an idea — as most all modern scholarship does — he would press still further to be grasped by its substance too. In other words, he was interested in both the idea and the experience that lay beneath it.

First, he would let the words of some great figure point toward something that mattered; then, not deigning to de-scribe it from there, he would try to move on into the ex-perience out of which it came, and from there speak of what he beheld. In this way, the words he used became an arena in which the listener could, if he or she so chose, experience something of the reality of those very ideas they and he were seeking to illuminate and understand.* His wife recollects:

> From my seat, I watched him walking around greeting friends, talking, asking questions, appearing clumsy and unsure about what he was going to say. He was certainly unimpressive — shabbily dressed and wearing strong glasses. I was anxious, fearing he might be unable to give a good lecture, but with his very first words at the podium, he was transformed. His voice rang out clearly; indecision had fled. He became the instrument of the powers of thought; *he was the word.* (H. Tillich, *From Time to Time,* Stein and Day, New York, p. 102.)

Tillich connected with life through *beholding.* As an individual, he gave his life to trying to see. In order to do this to the utmost he needed to get the fullest possible view of life and all existence. His *Systematic Theology,* which he undertook in 1925 at the outset of his career in Marburg, was what he built for himself to stand on. Sometimes the "little things" that people do have in them most of what one finds as well in the "big things" they do. Tillich went about building his system of thought in much the same way he built those incredible castlelike platforms, several feet high, when he went to the beach for a stay — with sloped ramps up them for easy walking up and down, and complete with drainage ditches to help withstand the onslaught of the elements. There he would sit, high atop his perch, and take in the invigorating expanse stretched out before

---

*Paul Tillich remained fond of the Pre-Socratics throughout his life, and it is little wonder, for his approach had much in common with, for example, Heraclitus', "Wisdom is one thing. It is to know the *thought* by which all things are steered through all things." H. Frankfort puts his finger on the significance of this: "Here, for the first time, attention is centered, not on the thing known, but on the knowing of it. Thought . . . controls the phenomena as it constitutes the thinker."

him. That is also the same function his system served. He of all people knew such things as this do not last forever, and so, when the rains of time began to wash it away near the end of his life, he did not try to pretend to himself or others that it was not happening. True to his chosen way, he would struggle even to take *that* fact into himself and go on from there.*

Finally, in October 1965 in a hospital in Chicago, Paul Tillich entered into the last major experience of his life: death. It began with the horror familiar to him: "Every thing is slipping away under my feet . . . " Showing the impulse most characteristic of him, and then checking himself in it, he said: " . . . let men not attempt to see what the gods cover with night and horror . . . " His wife, Hannah, listened for the next ten days as he recounted dreams, voiced new fears, and asked for her forgiveness; walking with him as he went ever farther and deeper into what was before him, until at last he came upon death face to face. At that point he made his way forward to meet it as he had always tried to meet the major realities of human existence before — moving to grasp as best he could that which was also grasping him.

> We cranked the bed up and held him, and then it happened — one gasping breath, the oxygen gurgled in his mouth, which was open. I held his hand . . . all of a sudden he let go, his body pranced as if in ecstacy, his bowels let go and his hand let go, he fell back . . . (H. Tillich, *From Time to Time*, pp. 221–24.)

---

*In his final lecture, the night before the severe heart attack from which he died ten days later, Tillich noted a principal shortcoming of his three-volume system and expressed his hope for the future of theology (*The Future of Religion*, p. 91). But he had already begun moving beyond his system in his later probing books, *Love, Power and Justice*, and *Morality and Beyond*.

Tillich had met the terminus, the utter end of life. It had been the life of one who wanted to know, one whose constant endeavor was to see what he could see. To behold is "to hold or keep in view, to watch; to regard or contemplate . . ." (OED). Beholding means fashioning one's "more" into a philosophic act and experience of life. And this is what Paul Tillich did supremely, as few others can, and he thrived on that as on nothing else.

> There are some among us for whom theoretical problems are existential, are matters of "to be, or not to be," because *theoria* means "looking at" things and being united with them in this way. My statements are primarily addressed to these. I myself belong to them. For us, the question of the cognitive encounter with reality, the question of the absolute and the relative in this encounter, is an existential concern — a concern that involves our whole existence. I should like it to be so for many, because ultimately knowing is an act of love. (P. Tillich, *My Search For Absolutes*, p. 83.)

Behesting: the Historical Experience of Life

> *Listen! A journalist is a person who writes history in the same moment that history happens. And it is the damn best way to write history.* — Oriana Fallaci

Roots are what we live from. We humans have two kinds: our biological roots that ground us in *what* we are, and our historical roots that ground us in *who.* Both arise out of the distant reaches of the past and sink their tentacles into the present, where alone we can draw the sustenance to mold ourselves and shape the future. We carry these roots with us wherever we go.

Our past and present are always with us. At any moment both are real. But they are not at all alike. To know who and what you came from is not enough to know who and what you are. To find this out you must go further. You must look at how you now do or do not take a stand — that is where you can see what you have and have not been so far.

For human beings, being human does not come naturally or easily. It comes hard, with effort, and is met with the greatest reluctance because being human means making choices and taking stands. That is what transforms human life into human lives, births the glory and tragedy of humankind, and starts all history — personal and universal. To read history is one thing, but to live historically is quite another. The essence of the latter lies in taking stands. Those who know this live differently from those who do not. They are the ones who resist oppression and thus struggle for freedom, who value will and hence keep alive the moral, and who, therefore, can see and know the heroic. One of these is Oriana Fallaci.

> I do not feel myself to be, nor will I ever succeed in feeling like, a cold recorder of what I see and hear. On every professional experience I leave shreds of my heart and soul; and I participate in what I see or hear as though the matter concerned me personally and were one on which I ought to take a stand . . . in fact, I always take one, based on a specific moral choice. (O. Fallaci, *Interview with History,* New York: Liveright Publishing, 1974, p. 9. The title shows that history is as alive for her as she is alive in it.)

In Europe Fallaci's name is a household word. She lives in Italy in a villa outside Florence. Her father helps her tend the vineyards there since she is so often away, roaming the world as an international correspondent for *L'Europeo.* She keeps an apartment in Manhattan to occasionally "live in" in her love affair with America, which no longer burns as brightly as it once did. Her articles appear in *Esquire, The New York Times Magazine* on Sundays, the *New Republic, Ms,* and in other magazines and newspapers at home and abroad. From time to time she is interviewed on national television. There are also her many books that, regardless of their focus, whether on warring nations, warring sexes, the space program, powerful and poignant novels, or tough interviews are filled with passages of what it means to be one who does not flinch either at being human or being alive.

In *If the Sun Dies,* written in 1967, Fallaci typically immersed herself in all aspects of what she was then working on: NASA and the U. S. space program — laughing, crying, sweating, hating, and loving her way through this science-fiction dream just then coming true, and one she believed was so crucial to the future of humankind — an assignment complete with von Braun, Willy Ley, Canaveral and Houston, Dee O'Hara (chosen as the astronauts' nurse because of her experience in obstetrics!); technical films; briefings on fuels and astronomy; John C. Lilly's work with dolphins on interspecies communication; scores of renowned scientists, technical experts and military officers; launching pads, countdowns, lift-offs; accidents and tragic pilot deaths; missile ranges and tracking stations — and after it all, found herself stopped cold by what she saw in the "third group" of astronauts turned out by NASA. So different were they from the original seven (Glenn, Shepard, Schirra, Grissom, Cooper, Slayton, Carpenter), that it seems as if they had skipped their thirties altogether, by jumping from their twenties to land in their mid-forties and full middle age. So she addressed them thus:

> Because I'm having fun in my thirties . . . I'm not dulling them with a precocious carbon-copy old age. . . . They're wonderful years . . . because they're free, rebellious, untrammeled, because the anguish of waiting is over, the melancholy of decline hasn't begun, because we're lucid, finally. . . . If we're religious, we're convinced of our religion. If we're atheists, we're convinced athiests

. . . we don't fear the mockery of the young because we're
young too, we don't fear the reproof of adults because
we're adults too . . . We are a field of ripened grain . . .
no longer green and not yet dried: lymph flows through
us at the right pressure, full of life, and our joy is alive,
and our grief is alive, we laugh and cry as we shall never
be able to again . . . so then why isn't it like this with you?
(*If the Sun Dies,* New York: Atheneum, 1967, p. 307)

This piece is typical. Her interviews are much like the
skirmishes in a fencing class as the instructor engages various students in mock matches throughout the floor. First,
the formal stance is assumed that begins the engagement.
There is that closely guarded, stalking and moving about
by both contestants. Soon the fledgling, sensing an opportunity, seizes the chance to score a point, and suddenly—
in a skillful motion that turns the other's movement to her
own advantage — the instructor executes a graceful
SSSSSWWWWWOOOOOOEEEEEEPP-THUNK that goes
right to the heart. And it is all over. The two contestants
know then just where things stand.

Yet there is more to Fallaci's interviews than finding out
where someone stands. Interviews that boil down to "so-
and-so said such-and-such about this-and-that" are only
half an inch above gossip columns. Try as one may it is
impossible to boil any Fallaci interview down to just that,
for she always gets at something much more: *the person
participating in the making of history.* That is something which
cannot be seen with the naked eye, nor can one take a
picture of a *person* or catch *history* on film, because when it
is developed both will be gone. Only the image remains, a
picture of someone doing something — but both the subject and subjects are gone. No machine or piece of equip-
ment can capture the subjectivity that makes history. It
always takes a person to reach the realm of the personal.

Those involved in history know that being a person is part of their trade.*

And what is this vibrant reality called *person?* It is biology making history into identity. It is being and becoming molded into a self. Person can neither be given nor taken, it can only be lived or died. Person and freedom are found together. You are not born a person, you become one; you are not born free, you must win freedom. Do not expect this to be easy or to meet with applause. Those who applaud it do not clap so much for you as for what they would like to be able to do themselves. Thus their applause is only a wish, which evaporates when it really counts, when it is time to take a stand — and so it counts for nothing. What does count are those who do not applaud, who do not need to wish because they already know, and who quietly stand with you. No, if you seek to become a person, then you must not only expect resistance, you must learn to thrive on it.

> Don't let yourselves be regimented by dogma, by uniforms, by doctrines, don't let yourselves be fooled by those who command you, by those who promise, who frighten, by those who want to replace one master with another, don't be a flock of sheep, for heaven's sake, don't hide under the umbrella of other people's guilt,

---

*Personal concern and involvement with issues has everything to do with history. As Allan Nevins wrote in *The Gateway to History:* "For above all, it is the historical point of view, the historical method of approach — *that is, the spirit of critical inquiry for the whole truth* — which, when applied to the past, makes history" (Garden City, Anchor Books, revised 1962).

And the English historian, R. G. Collingwood, pointed out in his autobiography, "We study history in order to see more clearly into the situation in which we are called upon to act. Hence the plane on which, ultimately, all problems arise is the plane of 'real' life: that to which they are referred for their solution is history." (*The Idea of History,* New York: Oxford University Press, 1970)

> think with your own brains, remember that each of you
> is somebody, a valuable individual, responsible, his own
> maker, defend your being, the kernel of all freedom,
> freedom is a duty, a duty even more than a right. (O.
> Fallaci, *A Man*, New York: Simon & Schuster, 1980, p.2)

Is it really this hard? Yes. Then is it worth the trouble?
You must consider the alternative and answer that for
yourself. But why is it like this? Because most people decide
to finish with life before life finishes with them. They start
to drift, and gradually begin to sink from the weight of
their own unspent vitality, until they come to settle in its
residue. And if you decide not to do this; if you choose to
take a stand that shows you will not join the hoards and
herds of the half-alive, then you have made it clear that
you will not go with them, that you will stand all by yourself
if necessary, and that will threaten them — and you will
have exposed them too, and that will anger them, and they
will see you as the enemy . . . and that is right. For if your
way prevails, theirs will die. And if their way prevails, you
will die. That is how it is and how it has always been.

To take a stand is to cut away from the crowd. Those
who do so never number more than a few and never like
crowds. If you do like crowds or if the crowd likes you —
beware, lest you sell your soul. Person and freedom are
always found together, but crowds and taking stands are
not. It is very hard to take a personal stand in a crowd.
Crowds try to work their way with numbers; crowds op-
press, and oppression survives in the world only because
the crowds do not resist it.

> I have always looked on disobedience toward the op-
> pressive as the only way to use the miracle of having been
> born. I have always looked on the silence of those who
> do not react or who indeed applaud as the real death of
> a woman or a man. And listen: for me the most beautiful
> monument to human dignity is still the one I saw on a

hill in the Peloponnesus. It was not a statue, it was not a
flag, but three letters that in Greek signify *No*. (O. Fallaci,
Interview with History, p. 13)

When one is moved, humanity is stirred, no matter how
slightly. To fail to stand up then for something one has
been stirred by kills the possibilities it may have offered for
a better way to live. Something is lost for everyone when a
person capitulates at the given hour. But to those who try,
though later it may seem like a floating island in some
uncharted sea which they are now at a loss to know where
it is or how to reach it again, they nevertheless will know
that once, for just a moment, they actually stood upon it
and felt its soil beneath their feet — even those will never
forget what it is like for a person to stand. Because of who
and what she is, Oriana Fallaci is deeply moved at the sight
of someone who has the dignity to stand and speak in the
face of impossible odds. To be so stirred, as she was here
and is still, is the surest sign that what she is stirred by is
in her too. It is a signal from her own soul. And it is in
these stirrings of the soul that we begin to discern that
movement in life which is *will*.

> Life, Francois, is a death sentence. But you're right not
> to tell me so. And just because we're condemned to death
> we must cross it well, we must fill it without wasting a
> step, without sleeping for a second, without being afraid
> of making mistakes or smashing ourselves — we who are
> men, not angels or beasts but men.*

And what would freedom be but empty if it did not have
within it the carrying out of what one wills? This movement

---

*Fallaci's words here run very much in the same vein as those of another
great solitary soul, Pascal: "It is dangerous to make man see too clearly
his equality with the brutes without showing him his greatness. It is also
dangerous to make him see his greatness too clearly apart from his
bruteness. It is still more dangerous to leave him in ignorance of both."

of will is what makes the self, and, eventually, a life. They arise out of the two most fundamental human choices of all: to do what one really wants to do, and not to do what one really wants to do — and both of these are acts of will. These acts make all human history what it is and isn't.

> Not by chance, if you are aware of it, does it consume you with a hundred feelings of inadequacy. Not by chance, when I find myself going through an event or an important encounter, does it seize me like anguish, a fear of not having enough eyes and ears and enough brains to look and listen and understand like a worm hidden in the wood of history. (O. Fallaci, *Interview with History*, p. 11.)

Other journalists marvel at what Fallaci is able to get out of an interview. When Mike Wallace, interviewed her for CBS's *60 Minutes,* he asked: "You're the only one who gets this special quality from — whether it is Henry Kissinger or Nguyen Van Thieu or the Shah of Iran. Why are you able to do this?" And she answered, "Because I do not go to them as a journalist . . . I am a person who goes to speak with another person sincerely curious, not in a superficial way. I really want to understand them." The reason she gets so much out of people is that she puts so much into life. She acts as the full person she is, with all her doubts, desires, arrogance and humility, hesitancy and brashness.

Those who live their humanity to the hilt never need to demand respect because they already command it. Their commanding presence is the direct result of their being so in command of their own person — and these are the ones who know the true magnitude and range of human responsibility. Their very lives summon others to account for what they have done or will do with theirs. A behest is a command, injunction, or bidding, and to behest formerly meant "to vow or promise" (OED). Behesting means fashioning one's "more" into an historical act and experience of life. Those who do this not only have a sense of history, and are thus able to write about it, but they can make and live it too. Only the few who are able to take a No are free to ask for any Yes in the world.

> But you had clearly understood it would end like this, and if ever you had a doubt, it vanished the moment you took the deep breath that sucked you to the other side of the tunnel: into the well where those who would like to change the world are regularly thrown, those who would like to bring down the mountain, give voice and dignity to the flock that bleats inside its river of fleece. The disobedient. The misunderstood and solitary. The poets. The heroes of senseless fables but without which life would have no meaning and to fight knowing that to lose would be pure madness. And yet for one day, that day that counts, that salvages, that often comes when you've given up hoping, and when it comes it leaves in the air a microscopic seed from which a flower will bloom: even the flock understood this, bleating within its river of fleece.

Besteading: the Political Experience of Life

> I am always mortified when anything is expected of me which I cannot fulfill.   — *Thomas Jefferson*

Those are clearly the words of someone with a passion for the useful — for finding it and being it. The touchstone of such people is to identify both what must be done and the way to do it; consequently, they are likely to be constantly on the lookout for these two things: the *ends* and the *means*.

The first, of course, is the stuff of politics, and the second is that of economics. Either one without the other leaves a good bit to be desired. Politics alone degenerates into a ceaseless plotting of interaffecting aims and influences, while economics dwindles to a continuous calculating of ever-shifting trends and commodities. But combine the two and it brings into being a critical mass from which explosive power can erupt; for when politics and economics merge so that ends and means can mix and intermingle, they then issue into *what you do with what you've got* — and that combination touches upon just about anything and everything that matters to humankind. It becomes, as we say, a "real going concern," one going on now as it has for as long as there have been people, and one which will go on for as long as there shall be.

Thomas Jefferson was a man very much given to both of these things, and that involved him in almost every issue of consequence to the people of his time. He was so involved, in fact, that the historian Henry Steele Commager considered him *the* central figure of American history — and if democracy should survive, then perhaps a central figure in all modern history as well.

Jefferson's life was lengthy, managed with exceptional deliberation, and crammed with achievement.* It is as if someone took aside a lad with an unusually receptive mind and said to him in somber tones at the most impressionable age possible, "Now the whole purpose of life is for you to make yourself useful."† To the very letter, that is what Thomas Jefferson did for eighty-three years.

---

*President John F. Kennedy, when honoring the Nobel Laureates at the White House in 1962, said that what he saw before him was " . . . probably the greatest concentration of talent in this house except for perhaps those times when Thomas Jefferson ate alone." (Adrienne Koch, *Jefferson*, Englewood Cliffs: Prentice Hall, 1971, p.1)

†Jefferson's father, whom he deeply admired, had taught the young Thomas to manage the farm, ride, plant, shoot, canoe, carpenter and do masonry, and judge livestock — all of which he began to do at age fourteen upon his father's death. What Peter Jefferson had said to

No man in this or any other country in the Western world — excepting only Leonardo da Vinci — ever matched Jefferson in the range of his activities, in the fertility of his thinking, and in the multiplicity of his interests. The number of things Jefferson did, or knew how to do, still astonishes. He was a mathematician, surveyor, architect, paleontologist, prosodist, lawyer, philosopher, farmer, fiddler, and inventor. He set up an educational system; he built a university; he founded a great political party; he helped design the national capitol; he was instrumental in establishing America's coinage; he doubled the territory of the United States; he invented machines and gadgets; he collected scientific materials in the fields of zoology, geology, and anthropology; he wrote a classic essay on poetry; he codified the legal system of his native State. Everything interested him; nothing was alien to his mind. (S. Padover, *Jefferson*, p. 7)

Over and above all that, Jefferson was a member of Congress, Governor of Virginia, Ambassador to France, Secretary of State, Vice President and twice President of the United States, author of the Religious Freedom Act of Virginia and primary author of the Declaration of Independence. In addition, he managed to exchange a staggering 50,000 personal letters (Betts & Bear, *The Family Letters of Thomas Jefferson*, Columbia, MO: University of Missouri Press, 1970, p.1).

People given to the useful and the effective carry *what could be* around inside themselves like an unwrapped package — and they are generally happiest when occupied in getting that package opened — the sooner the better. When their mind's eye has seen how to do something they believe ought to be done, then things already appear to be some-

---

his son time and again was: "Never ask another to do for you what you can do for yourself." (Saul K. Padover, *Jefferson*, New York: Mentor, 1970, p. 10) what behind schedule, which is why such people often in-dicate a slight impatience. These pilgrims of the possible are so interested in working out some practical future, that they seldom take note of the past, experiencing it mostly as something that is simply over, whereas the present is always here for getting on with whatever can be gotten to *now*. (It is interesting to note that Jefferson kept no diary, and upon retirement from the Presidency wrote in a letter that nothing could be more repugnant to him than to write the history of his life. Years later, at age seventy-seven, he tried writing his autobiography, but after about sixty pages he noted, "I am already tired of talking about myself," and soon abandoned the whole undertaking.)

Yet if you focus on what these people *do,* instead of on what they themselves focus upon, you will probably see little more than a blur of activity or a glint from their awards and achievements. What sustains them lies off in the dis-tance, and their daily deeds, burdensome and overly in-dustrious as they may appear to others, throb with the enlivening satisfaction of getting at least a piece of tomor-row started today. Nor should one expect to find their hearts beating in their usually well-ordered minds. For to them the mind, akin to the chief executive's staff, is only the more visible and accessible attendant to the real manager of it all. To reach this center, the true core, one must find that particular merging of ends and means by which each such person is both motivated and oriented. Frequently this will take the form of some dream or vision, one which sometimes remains wrapped up inside the person forever. Jefferson, however, found the string, untied it, and let loose a dream of that by which all humans had a right to live:

> . . . under the law of nature, all men are born free, and every one comes into the world with a right to his own

person, which includes the liberty of moving and using it at his own will. (*Howell v. Netherland*, April 1770.)*

. . . We hold these truths to be self-evident: that all men are created equal; that they are endowed by their Creator with inherent and inalienable rights; that among these are life, liberty, and the pursuit of happiness; that to secure these rights, governments are instituted among men, deriving their just powers from the consent of the governed; that whenever any form of government becomes destructive of these ends, it is the right of the people to alter or abolish it . . . (*The Declaration of Independence*, 1776.)†

. . . Almighty God hath created the mind free . . . the opinions of man are not the object of civil government, nor under its jurisdiction; . . . that to suffer the civil magistrate to intrude his powers into the field of opinion and to restrain the profession or propogation of principles, on the supposition of their ill tendency, is a dangerous fallacy, which at once destroys all religious liberty . . . (*Act for Establishing Religious Freedom*, 1786.)

. . . it is a heavenly comfort to see that these principles are yet so strongly felt . . . I pray God that these principles may be eternal.‡

---

*As a young lawyer turning twenty-six, Jefferson is here defending a mulatto seeking freedom in Virginia. Arguing against George Wythe, who taught him law, Jefferson's remarks were found to be so radical that the judge cut short his argument and ruled against the defendant slave.

†Written at the age of thirty-three, this is his original draft, which the Continental Congress altered only by striking "inherent and" and putting "certain" in their place.

‡Quoted from Bernard Mayo, *Jefferson Himself*, Charlottesville: University Press of Virginia, 1973.

He held to this dream until the end of his life, writing the first statement here in his mid-twenties and the last at age eighty. Making it come true was the task for his head. Like so many stirred by the Enlightenment, his mind was metamorphosed into that of a work horse to plow a given plot of ground until time and toil would produce a crop of *principles* to then harvest and put to use. These were usually seen as blendings of ends and means which, when sufficiently grasped, would enable the attentive individual to perform the essential operations of mathematics, masonry, music, or whatever. Little wonder, therefore, that Jefferson gravitated to law, a field that consists mainly of the pursuit and application of the principles involved in the case at hand, and an enterprise that could afford him a double-barreled satisfaction he would not likely find elsewhere.

It is a common mistake to assume that much head means little heart. Jefferson was well aware of that too:

> Let the gloomy monk, sequestered from the world, seek unsocial pleasures in the bottom of his cell! Let the sublimated philosopher grasp visionary happiness, while pursuing phantoms dressed in the garb of truth. Their supreme wisdom is supreme folly; and they mistake for happiness the mere absence of pain. Had they ever felt the solid pleasure of one generous spasm of the heart, they would exchange for it all the frigid speculations of their lives . . . (B. Mayo, *Jefferson Himself,* p. 137.)

These words show someone who can think *and* feel, and those who would pry the head and heart of this man apart will only end up with a picture that distorts the life he actually lived. To see just how pronounced this other side of his life was, one only need look at his obvious love for his wife, Martha, and at the intensity of his grief at her early death; the extent of his caring for his daughters; his earlier sentiments for Rebecca Burwell as well as his attraction to the married Betsy Walker (the latter being sensationalized to the point of national scandal after he became President); his deep involvement with the lovely Maria Cosway after he was widowed and had become Ambassador to France; and finally his extremely close and lasting relationship with Sally Hemmings. On the other hand, however, those recognizing the signs of passion in Jefferson — amorous, political, for Nature, and, indeed, even for poetry (as in Macpherson's *Ossian* and elsewhere) — and taking them to mean the same as they do today, overlook the differences between our time and his, and they too will fail to see his life for what it really was. Suffice it to say he was subjected to forceful tugs and pulls throughout his life, and the conflict he felt between head and heart was only one more conflict in the life of a man accustomed to living with several.

To be sure, the composure of Jefferson's life was considerable, but that was because the swirls it was called upon to contain were considerable too. The inward and the outward influence each other, and an individual's life turns on its axis as a movement of the two. Generally, Jefferson managed to intermingle the formidable aims and influences of his life remarkably well, but there were a few occasions when the control required to maintain his finely balanced rotation so overtaxed his mental powers that it would leave him with a headache which lasted for days. These were usually periods of identifiable stress during which, in the throes of personal or situational conflict, he sought for some slim pass over which he could safely cross without tumbling into the consuming extremes that always lay at either side.

In living life this way, everything hinges on being "in control," which has little to do with domination and everything to do with *managing to find the means*. Again, the best way to accomplish this life-sustaining task is by discovering and applying all pertinent principles. That is what keeps the whole system running and going. In essence, this is the act of governing; it is government in operation, whether it be of the nation or of the self. In fact, to Jefferson, the government of the nation began with the government of the self. To govern oneself is to be free. That is why government and freedom become inextricably linked, and preserving this crucial union hinges on the ongoing ability to find the means. Jefferson personally valued this specific ability very highly, writing that it was " . . . part of the American character to consider nothing as desperate, to surmount every difficulty by resolution and contrivance. In Europe there are shops for every want; its inhabitants, therefore, have no idea that their wants can be supplied otherwise. Remote from all other aid, we are obliged to invent and to execute; to find means within ourselves, and not to lean on others" (B. Mayo, *Jefferson Himself*, p. 118).

The three things that Jefferson wished to be remembered for all had to do with *finding the means:* the Declaration of Independence established means to pursue the principles of self-government; the Statute of Virginia for Religious Freedom provided means of applying the principles he saw as necessary to preserve the freedom of opinion; and the University of Virginia was a means of continuing the ongoing pursuit and application of both these and other valued principles. Each of these constituted a means to help achieve the ends of freedom. His life shows a soul always seeking to, as he put it, "fix in the principles" that mattered to him most, so that what he envisioned could be made to work.*

---

*This abiding trait of Jefferson's shows itself in something he wrote when still in his twenties — " . . . I answer, everything is useful which contributes to fix in the principles and practices of virtue" — and is also visible in what he penned once while in his eighties: "The University will give employment to my remaining years, and quite enough for my senile faculties. It is the last act of usefulness I can render, and could I see it open I would not ask an hour more of life." (B. Mayo, p. 28 and p. 336)

Being interested in making things work is but a step away from a basic curiosity in *how* things work, which often manifests itself in a special fondness for tools and gadgets of every kind. Those who possess this curiosity learn quickly how this or that should be done, and are therefore easily enticed at the prospect of lending a hand to get the show on the road by making something work. If the matter or issue before them is important enough, then chances are good that such individuals can be totally lured into the fray — at least until the major obstacle is cleared, the riddle is solved, or the missing piece of the puzzle is found. Jefferson was lured like this more than once after he abandoned public life, and for him the underlying issue was always to make the grand dream work. As he reflected: "Nature intended me for the tranquil pursuits of science, by rendering them my supreme delight. But the enormities of the times in which I have lived have forced me to take part in resisting them, and to commit myself on the boisterous ocean of political passions" (D. Malone, *Jefferson the President*, V, Boston: Little, Brown, 1974 p. 668).

> The station which we occupy among the nations of the earth is honorable, but awful . . . Trusted with the destinies of this solitary republic of the world, the only monument of human rights, and the sole depository of the sacred fire of freedom and self-government, from hence it is to be lighted up in other regions of the earth. . . . All mankind ought then, with us, to rejoice in its prosperity, and sympathize in its adverse fortunes, as involving everything dear to man . . . to preserve from all danger this hallowed ark of human hope and happiness. (D. Malone, *Jefferson the President*, V, p. 667.)

Solving an issue at large can, curiously, leave it unsolved at home. Jefferson kept slaves at Monticello for as long as he lived, although opportunities presented themselves, soliciting his support in ventures aimed at extending liberty to ever-widening spheres, such as the courageous proposal put forward by Frances Wright, who sought to use her fortune to create a community where blacks and whites could live together in a manner truly integrated, educated, and free. Weakened by months of extreme illness, and now nearing death, Jefferson nevertheless gave a response indicating that even at the end of his life it was a struggle for him to resist the abiding inclination to make himself useful:

> At the age of eighty-two, with one foot in the grave, and the other uplifted to follow it, I do not permit myself to take part in any new enterprises, even for bettering the condition of man, not even the great one which is the subject of your letter, and which has been through life that of my greatest anxieties. The march of events has not been such as to render its completion practicable within the limits of time alloted to me; and I leave its accomplishment as the work of another generation. . . . The abolition of the evil is not impossible; it ought never therefore to be despaired of. Every plan should be adopted, every experiment tried, which may do something towards its ultimate object. (F. Brodie, *Thomas Jefferson: An Intimate History*, New York: Bantam, 1975, pp. 625–26)

To bestead is "to be of service or use to; to avail" (OED). Besteading means fashioning one's "more" into a political or economic act and experience of life. Near the end of his life, Jefferson could draw some consolation from the fact that the means he had helped to create were all beginning to work. Writing of the Declaration of Independence, he believed it

> . . . will be (to some parts sooner, to others later, but finally to all), the signal of arousing men to burst the chains under which monkish ignorance and superstition had persuaded them to bind themselves, and to assume the blessings and security of self-government. That form which we have substituted, restores the free right to the

unbounded exercise of reason and freedom of opinion. All eyes were opened, or opening, to the rights of man. The general spread of the light of science has already laid open to view the palpable truth, that the mass of mankind has not been born with saddles on their backs, nor a favored few booted and spurred, ready to ride them legitimately, by the grace of God. (B. Mayo, *Jefferson Himself,* p. 345)

A few days after writing this, he died. Like his close friend John Adams, he desired to live to the fourth of July. A little before midnight on July 3, 1826, Jefferson inquired of Nicholas Trist, his granddaughter's husband, "This is the Fourth?" The next morning Trist wrote to his brother:

He has been dying since yesterday morning, and till twelve o'clock last night, we were in momentary fear that he would not live, as he desired, to see his own glorious Fourth.*

Both Thomas Jefferson and John Adams made it to July 4, the day of that dream they and others began to unfold when they had announced fifty years earlier that they were bringing into being something new. Jefferson had given his life to creating those means which others might use to achieve the end of a freedom also meant to be theirs.

Belonging: the Scientific Experience of Life

The more the organism perceives itself the less we have to debate about truth. Much becomes self-evident in the process of living. — Stanley Keleman

Once every now and then, somebody stumbles upon an exposed piece of something ancient, digs away the dirt of

---

* Adams's last words were, "Thomas Jefferson still survives." (F. Brodie, *Thomas Jefferson,* p. 633)

centuries and finds a door, pushes it open, and there discovers a hidden or long-buried part of human life. Then our views are changed and a new experience of life begins to sprout. Sprouts, by the way, have a lot in common with life. They are both strong and delicate at the same time, and so all-of-one-piece that when you pick their tops you pull their roots; yet, tender and tiny as they are, they can survive most anything. Ever see a spread of sprouts get trampled on?

Whoever uncovers a door and gets it open, is likely to continue going in and out of it to deepen the discovery and show others the way they can do the same. Stanley Keleman made just such a find and spends his life doing this very thing.

Born of immigrant parents from Hungary and Romania, Keleman grew up in Brooklyn. His athletic prowess won him scholarships to a number of colleges, but he nevertheless turned away from the path most others would have followed because . . .

> . . . the answers he wanted were not to be found in the academy. . . . His suspicion . . . led him to the out-of-the-way institutions. . . . His teachers were all outlaws who denied the orthodox wisdom of the day: problems of the mind were to be dealt with by psychiatrists and problems of the body by physicians, and never the twain would meet . . . *

To find what others have not found, one must seek as others have not sought. This is risky and most who try it end up finding nothing, getting lost, or both; but Keleman, ever one of the few, did not. Not only did he find what he

---

*Sam Keen, who interviewed Keleman for *Psychology Today* and has conducted seminars and workshops with him, writes: "Stanley Keleman is a celebrant of biological life. If we had Earthfathers, he might be one." (From Keen's *Voices and Visions,* New York: Harper & Row, 1974, p. 154)

was looking for, he made his way back as well. In this he brings to mind the central figure in those stories who hears an old legend about some wondrous lost place, a sun-filled valley all green and growing, where life thrives as nowhere else on earth, but which is far away and surrounded by perilous hazards and dangers nobody dares to venture into. The main character, remarkably average in every respect except for believing the tale to be true, sets out to find the place and is thus seen by everyone else as foolhardy or downright crazy. Encountering hardships unmet before, and suffering losses never to be regained, the seeker eventually becomes lost and ultimately reaches the limit where there is neither anything to go on with nor enough left to get back, where all that remains is the final act of giving in and collapsing — and, right then and there, discovers it is all just as the legend described. Of course the temptation is to remain in that idyllic place forever, and some versions of the story make it clear that those who leave can never return again; so, a few in the party elect to remain, but the strongest, those most whole, are willing to jeopardize all to make the long trek back.

What a stunning sameness there is between such stories and what it is to find the Self and reach one's soul. The ones who do this keep it from then on, even if they come back. Of course the recountings are scoffed at by those who do not leave their habitat and habits of home, for they can only hear these as fanciful tales which do not relate to anything they know as real. Nevertheless, those who return have a look about them, a certain unaccountable manner, which the skeptical stay-at-homers cannot explain, and which, in moments when they are alone and have nothing else on their minds, visits them to make them wonder if maybe there is something to it after all.

Keleman has these marks. His words and ways show that he underwent an experience such as this, seeking what so many myths and legends are all about, finding that greater wholeness of life, and making it back to show others a way they can get there on their own.

> In the early part of my life, I sought a source of authority, a reference, a philosophy from which I could find values and purpose that would serve as a conduit for my energies. Many of the values of my culture at that time were unacceptable to me. They were either mechanistic, low-level materialism or a pathetic religious dogma that was no longer historically applicable. My feeling of awe and curiosity about the beginnings of things and the nature of existence found no home either in the world of science or in the images of the Orient.
>
> . . . I began to have a whole range of experiences, which encompassed past and present, ideas and needs, thinking and feeling, urges to act and urges to wait, archetypal pictures and emotions, inner and outer space and time.
>
> . . . I felt at home in this world of many dimensions, but of course this being at home was fraught with anxieties. I thought at the time that the strangeness I experienced was due to the releasing of old conflicts and energies that I had to resolve and become accustomed to. This was in line with then contemporary psychological thought. It was not until much later that I knew that I had stepped outside the realm of our society's knowledge. We had no tradition of living a bodily life. (S. Keleman, *Somatic Reality*, Berkeley: Center Press, 1979, pp. 9–11)

The lowly *body*, which even St. Francis had referred to as "Brother Ass" — was this piece of common clay able to lead anyone on to a fresher view or a more whole experience of life?

> I don't deal with interpersonal relationships. I deal with your relationship to yourself, with helping you into more intimate connection with yourself — by working directly with your body. The way your body is, *is* the way you are. That is my working principle.
>
> System-oriented scientists who need to see the body as

a machine, in terms of genetic code, feedback systems, organ organization and biochemical systems with predictable programs, do not seem to grasp that life includes mechanics, that it is living that is structured — that structure is a living function. (S. Keleman, *The Human Ground: Sexuality, Self and Survival,* Berkeley: Center Press, 1975, p. 20)

If Keleman is right about prevalent attitudes toward the body, then what he is saying will strike most people as making far too much of much too little. We in the West especially have persisted for centuries in making a molehill out of the mountain which the body truly is; and a mountain of meanings is exactly what Stanley Keleman sees whenever he looks at some*body*. He can discern more of an individual's character in how one speaks, stands, sits, and moves about, than many psychologists ever glean from full batteries of personality instruments, projection tests, and other diagnostic tools and techniques. This is not so much an indictment of the "state of the art" of psychology, as it is an indication of the significance of what Keleman is working with and his genius at doing so.

Who you are as you stand in front of me is who you are in the world, is how you perceive the world, is exactly how you have learned to deal with the world. Your past in hereditary as well as personal terms is living at this present moment as you the body. (S. Keleman, *The Human Ground,* pp. 19–20)*

---

*Do not mistake Keleman's approach for any of the popularized versions of the "body language" phenomenon which erroneously leads people to imagine that every gesture is infused with a general but latent meaning. The one who has studied this aspect of life more carefully and in greater detail than anyone else reminds us, "I must emphasize that no position, expression, or movement ever carries meaning in and of itself." (R. L. Birdwhistell, *Kinesics and Context: Essays on Body Motion Communication* (Philadelphia: University of Pennsylvania Press, 1970, pp. 44–45)

One might assume this boils down to saying: the mind and the body are one. But doesn't everybody already know this? All it takes is a look around to see for yourself what every*body* knows. You may feel foolish doing this because at first you will only notice what you regularly see; however it does not take very long to spot that split between thought and action for which *Homo sapiens* is famous. Do not stop with that, though, but go on to look a little more closely. Can you make out how the body not only shows the split, but gives signs of the particular kind of thinking and doing that makes it up? If you cannot, then try again a few times. Paying attention to this very separation in yourself may provide some good clues of what to look for.

Practice looking at and seeing things this way for about one week and it will already start to make less and less sense to regard the "mind" as one matter and the "body" as another. And for all our sophisticated stressing of things psychosomatic, most of the dominant views of human life found in our culture still reduce mind or body to the one or the other. It is easy enough to say a unity exists between the two, but the final test of actually holding this view is to be able to see it right before one's eyes. Keleman does this, genuinely joining both in an organismic whole wherein the body is always speaking its mind — and this view opens the door to a broader approach to and deeper participation in the reality of our living and dying.* This underlying view is evident in a string of unpolished sayings that show the man at work.

> The *How* — we shall pursue this relentlessly. How do
> you do what you do physically? This will discourage all

---

*Keleman's growing number of books clearly reflect this overall description of his view, two of which bear the titles *Your Body Speaks Its Mind*, New York: Pocket Books, 1976, and *Living Your Dying*, New York: Random House/Bookworks, 1974.

psychologizing, and will restore to you the experience of yourself . . . No self-formation is possible unless you start by experiencing who and what you are . . . Behavior is always predictable, but growth never is . . . "Feeling" is not a great answer in itself, but some have as their profession getting you to do this. What we think is a "thought" or "feeling" is, literally, something we are doing . . . All of the body methods — and I know them all — pride themselves in non-verbalness. This is contempt for humanness. We think words even if we don't speak them . . . Growth is never an explosion. It is a symphony of forces pushing you . . . Every contraction is a statement of making one's boundaries somewhere and is an alternative to collapsing . . . Endings signal that which has outlived its usefulness and which we must change our relationship to. Conflict is not so much what is going on between you and me, but has to do with what is ending and beginning in either or both of us . . . The split called "body-mind" is nothing more than a perception of where the charge is . . . Self-repeating and self-experiencing are both very important; they are the two ways. If you know this, you can tell when you are tending the garden and when you are seeing the stars . . . I am always unified. When am I not? When I *describe* myself as not unified. That is why I push for the *How,* because a person will begin to describe how connected he or she is. The real question is how are you connected to yourself. (From the author's notes at a workshop given by Keleman in 1974.)

Despite his conceptualizations, it is not accurate to portray Keleman as one who proffers intellectual views; quite the contrary, he labors and watches as people are enlivened in flesh and blood, muscle and bone — and that is where one must look to witness who this man is and to see what he really does. An instance of this, taken from the occasion on which he made the remarks just quoted, provides a sample of what it is like when Keleman steps into the central arena of his life and work.

It happened in the summer of 1974 during an intensive three-week course entitled "The Life of the Body" held at the University of California in Berkeley. About fifty-five people were there, coming mostly from the United States, with a few from Italy, France, Denmark, Germany, and Canada. There was the normal silence following the period of information and illustration, and most participants were privately sifting through what had been said and sorting out some piece that applied to them personally.

"Anyone have anything they want to say?" asked Stanley.

Almost everyone lowered their heads.

"I do" a woman said suddenly, and all eyes turned her way, happy to have something to do. She sat erect, a rather short woman of very solid build, probably in her fifties. Her medium-length dark blond hair was kept in place as neatly as she herself seemed to be. Her manner was friendly yet formal, like that of those who regularly deal with the public in a politely civil way.

"It's a dream I just had" she continued. "I dreamed I was asleep and awoke to discover my house was burning. All I could think of was that I had to move fast to get my family out safely. I shouted to wake them, but as we ran out into the hall I saw the front door was blocked by a wall of flame; so I looked around, and there at the other end of the hallway was a door I never noticed before; not a door in my real house, but it was in my dream. It was metal, and when I put my hands on it it burned them."

Here she let her eyes take in some of the others in the group who by this time were all watching her every move, and then she looked back at Keleman.

"You know," she went on, gesturing toward the back of her neck and shoulders, which had a thickness that did not look muscular so much as tightly packed, "I've always felt like I had a lot of strength up in this part of my body; and in my dream I thought if I used all that to push the door as hard as I could, that I'd get it open and we'd all be safe. I tried, but it didn't budge; then — I really ssshhhuuuuvvved it — and it opened. And so I got everybody out, but my dog died in the fire. So . . . it wasn't what you'd call a happy dream, but somehow it was still a good dream."

The dream needed no interpretation, but most leaders would have moved right then to do that. Everyone could hear it came out of a life where old ways were being sealed off and coming to an end; and finding new ways would require a considerable expenditure of strength if they were to keep loved ones linked together — and that in undertaking to make the passage, dear things would be lost forever. Keleman just sat there, eyeing the woman closely, letting the meaning of what she had presented start to leaven the whole lump of both her own life and also that of the group. When the significance had visibly seeped to the core, and thawed it, Stanley made his move.

"Ever been to a revival?" he said surprisingly.

"Why, aahhh, no."

"Oh" shrugged Keleman, as if about to leave the matter, but leaving instead an opportunity for the taking, which she lost no time in reaching for.

"But it is strange you should ask because . . . " she said, looking the way one does when some consciously concealed part of oneself has suddenly surfaced and is now capable of being seen and shown, " . . . because a hymn has been going through my head."

"Would you like to sing it?" he invited.

"Oh no." she said so softly that only those close by could hear. "Besides, I'm not sure I know the words."

"I bet *he* knows the words;" said Keleman, indicating the man next to her who happened to be a priest. "Go ahead and sing; he'll join you."

She started out in a very faint and quivery voice with the

words: "Let us break bread together, Hallalu . . . ". All at once she stood up straight, and looking around in the manner of someone ready to do business, she continued: "What I'd like to do is really *sing* this." Now her voice was starting to gather much more resonance and a touch of exuberance as she then turned to stand up in her chair, as if to say she wanted this to be seen by all the world. " . . . I mean sing it out loud; and just let everybody join in who wants to; . . . Let us break bread together, Hallalu. Let us break bread together, Hallalu."

As her voice flowed like a fountain through her vocal chords, the sound coming deep from within her, she started to clap her hands — and others in the group began to do the same. Some whose English had not been able to keep up with the pace, and who had turned to others for a translation, now sensed what was happening, and most of them got on their feet to fully participate in what was now unfolding. When life intervenes this way, the only choice is to participate or to observe. There is no middle way.

Meanwhile, Stanley, who was standing and clapping at his seat, leaned over to better hear what one of the more brilliant intellectuals began to say: "Stanley, that was beautiful. And the way you handled it when she . . . "

Interrupting without rudeness the laudatory comments being placed like a laurel wreath upon his head, Keleman said, still clapping, "God never therapizes — just heals." Then he turned and walked away.

The aim here is clear: *to unite as fully as possible with the realness of life.* The effects of this are obviously therapeutic, but what is equally obvious is that all this involves much more than what is generally termed "therapy." Keleman resists using this word as a label for what he does:

> I don't see what I do as therapy. I dislike the idea of fixing which the word "therapy" suggests. It does not communicate what happens between me and people I

work with. The words grounding, opening, and participating, connecting vital responsiveness, seem appropriate.* (S. Keleman, *The Human Ground,* p. 27)

And what *are* we to call one who has such a goal and
works in this way? In the Greece of Socrates' time and for
some centuries afterward, especially at that marvelous center of Greco-Roman learning which thrived at the Museum
and Library in Alexandria, there is no doubt about it at all:
Keleman would have been called a philosopher (a term he
has used on occasions to refer to himself). But that was
when philosophy and science worked side by side and still
spoke to one another. Part of this tradition survived in
Europe up to the very end of the nineteenth century,
though by that time it had come to use the word "science"
more to describe itself.†

The one question science asks more than any other as it
gazes at the Universe is *How?* How is such and such possible? How does this or that come to be? This is the very
question Keleman most consistently asks of life and seeks
to answer. How if life formed? How does it function? How
does this person, or that one, come to be the way they are?
It is only among the most genuinely dedicated scientists
that one will find the zealous respect for "the natural order

---

*When that basic whole, which every individual is, is broken down into
a "problem" that is then to be "worked through" by means of a particular
"therapeutic method" in order to achieve an "outcome" which has been
somewhat arbitrarily defined as "healthy," then those who split up both
the *process* of therapy and the *person* of those involved in it (including
that of the therapist) in this way, are likely to succeed only in dividing
"therapists" into the-rapists instead.

†At the end of the 19th century the German word for science, *Wissen-
shaft,* meant almost exactly what Plato and Aristotle meant by "philosophy." Since then the meaning of both words has undergone a
considerable change in which there is a mixture of both gain and loss
(see Windelband's *A History of Philosophy,* I, New York: Harper Torch-
books, 1958, pp. 1–2)

of things" that Keleman has. To experience life with the soul of a scientist is to be so convinced that part and whole belong together, that one's life is given to a continuing clarification of how the two fit together and relate to one another. The part and the whole of science, and the one and the many of philosophy, are closely related. To belong is "to be connected with in various relations" (OED). Belonging means fashioning one's "more" into a scientific act and experience of life.

> . . . we're part of an evolution toward a new subjectivity. We are moving, as a culture, further and further away from the old scientific, distanced way of making objects of the world. We are moving toward more participation in it. (S. Keleman, *Living Your Dying*, pp. 139–40.)

Stanley Keleman is still on his most basic expedition: to make his way on to a new science of life itself.

These, then, are modes of human becoming. They may not be the only ones but they are most certainly major ones, for they continuously recur throughout human existence. Their significance is enormous because they constitute fundamentally different ways of comprehending life as well as pursuing it. Thus they serve to give us a glimpse of some of the most profound dimensions and distinctions found in the human soul.

In the course of time every person develops a way of experiencing life that becomes characteristic of him or her. Friends readily spot this as that person's ways of thinking, feeling, tending, judging, perceiving, sensing, and intuiting, and it is in the totality made up of these that one can see the overall configuration of an individual soul.

THE DIS-EASES AND DISEASES OF THE SOUL

Now that we have seen that *soul* is the unique totality of each individual, it is easy to understand why all experience affects the soul. Our life and all there is to it, from the base and basic to the very refined, comes and goes through the soul. Every human need touches the soul and each one of these needs is experientially elaborated by it. When we detect these as "dis-eases" within us, they often help direct our lives; but when we do not, they can grow into full-fledged diseases by which we are disfigured and our whole lives are distorted.

WHAT YOUR BEING IS BECOMING

Since the soul is the essence of a whole life it can also be defined in another way. *Your soul is what your being is becoming.* Without the reality of the soul there would be no such thing as "a life"; it would simply be a series of successions with nothing constant at the core.

Amidst life's changes, with its many beginnings and endings, the soul abides and runs from start to finish through it all. When you take a life and add it up or boil it down, what it all comes to is the soul — which is always too much to explain but never too big to experience. And because it is alive and real we can actually experience our soul and come to know it.

WHO You have Been and Are Becoming

ISSUE: *The Soul's Relating.* There are three basic ways of relating one's life to others and to the world:

(1)   to share most of what matters with another person,

(2)   to share pieces of what matters with several people,

(3)   to do neither of these and keep things mostly to oneself.

IDENTIFICATION: (A) Which of these three has been your fundamental way of relating yourself to the world so far? (B) After years of relating in one way, many people shift to relating in another — though this may happen so gradually that it goes unnoticed for a long while or is attributed to external factors alone (changes in work or duties, friends moving away, new and engrossing involvements, etc.). Are there any indications of such a shift in your life now? Do you think you will continue relating as you have in the past, or do you see a change in store?

WHAT Directs and Distorts Your Life

ISSUE: *The Soul's Elaborating* — What happens to anybody happens to the soul. Whatever is done to the body is done to the soul. It registers all of our experience, and so through the soul one can "take the pulse" of his or her life.

IDENTIFICATION: (A) Gaze on how the basic human needs are elaborated by the soul. Then try to determine the particular way in which you experience and handle all of these. Recall instances that are specific and vivid enough to bring your response to each need into focus. (B) Which needs are you inclined to underindulge or overindulge? (C) What does your current profile look like? What dis-eases or disfigurations are you able to detect now? Where are you strongest and where are you weakest? What direction does this suggest for your life in the near furture? What step could you take right now *and* . . . what difference would it make if you did?

WHEN It Is Time to Live Differently

ISSUE: *The Soul's Willing* — When one can tell that one has no real living room, then it is time to make a change. Some signs of this are when one's interests and energies dwindle to next to nothing, and when one's life no longer runs up and down over rough places and smooth with long stretches of plain inbetween — but instead bounces from side to side, back and forth on a track that runs from boredom at one end to anger at the other.

IDENTIFICATION: (A) Two basic rules that apply to all human life are: (1) people do only what they really want to do, and (2) people don't do what they really want to do. Everyone's life is a mixture of both of these acts. *First,* let come to mind a time when you did something you very much wanted to do. *Second,* identify something you once wanted to do (and perhaps still want to do) but have never done. *Third,* try to determine two things you have not done but believe you would like to — one in the area of work and another in your relationships. (B) See if you can gather from your actual behavior in the past whether you are more of a *niche-filler* or a *niche-maker*. Both are ways of being productive; however the creative energies of the first are spent mostly in *finding* the right niche, while those of the second are given mostly to *fashioning* it. (C) If it appears for the most part that you are using your energy to make a place to use your energies — and if you genuinely *care* about where you are located or working at present — then you might try to restructure things where you already are. It's not *having* a boss that makes most jobs unbearable; it's having to do things his or her way — *that* is what takes most of the life out of it.

WHERE the Living Waters Flow

ISSUE: *The Soul's Creating and Re-Creating* — The modes of human becoming are distinct ways of knowing and participating in life. The waters of each run deep, are quite different, and do not taste at all the same. To find "where the living water flows" one must go to the place where a particular well is and learn to draw from it. It is easy to dip a hand in all wells and drink from their surface, but most of us can draw deeply from only one or two. Yet that is more than enough to sustain the creativity in a life and to regularly refresh one's soul.

IDENTIFICATION: (A.) Look again at the various modes of becoming. Prioritize the list to reflect the mode or modes that are most important for you, and then run all the way down to the one that matters least to you. (B.) Were there any times in your life when you were affected by some of these modes in ways that indicate interests and abilities related to them that you may not have thought about before? Where do you suppose you acquired your chief modal inclinations? Were you, perhaps, influenced by others whom you admired or respected? As you now look back, was the influence appropriate or inappropriate — does it seem based on the deepest and most natural tendencies of your life or not? (C.) It is not necessarily desirable to make one's most important modal interests the central focus of one's career. Many people earn their living doing something unrelated to what deeply moves or stirs them, and yet effectively find avocational outlets that keep their creativity alive and their energies replenished. How have you chosen to go about mixing both the necessary and the nourishing? Is it working or is the cost so great that it needs to be reexamined and possibly rearranged?

WHY Answer if There is a Question in Your Soul?

ISSUE: *The Soul's Wondering and Waiting* — It is a great mistake to become so answer-oriented that you miss the importance of finding the questions. Most worthwhile discoveries of humankind result from someone putting the question in a different way. (Einstein, for example,was led to his findings by asking what it would be like if one could ride a beam of light.) The best teachers are those whose answers keep the questioning alive. We should be wary of any and all who suggest that they have The Answer. Anyone you make your answer will very soon become your problem.

IDENTIFICATION: Why seek to answer when there is a deeper question in your soul? Live the question and let it speak — and it probably will. If you come across someone who seems to have found the answer to what you have been looking for, see if you can discover the questioning which got them there. Maybe it could work for you as well. If not, then set out on your own to find an answer that will.

The more the experiencing, the greater the soul; the fuller the life, and the fewer the words about it. Experience alone will not "save" the soul, but it may well lead to the recovery of it. And that is important enough all by itself, because the soul is what enables one to sense the spirit.

·7·

SENSING THE SPIRIT

Spirit is life cutting into itself.   — *Nietzsche*

AT ANY MOMENT

Spirit is a reality even harder to grasp than soul. It involves all that we have touched on so far, and more. While soul is seen in a life's full sweep, spirit can be sensed only in its moments. It comes and goes, it is free and also freeing, and its moments stand out and remain special forever. At any moment in life it can intervene — and it does.

Spirit is the soul meeting and being met by the power of life anew. Acts of spirit open life up to the soul, but it is costly for that to occur. We never meet spirit as an object or content but only as power, as something which stirs and moves us like nothing else. Therefore we do not usually recognize it at the time but afterward, only as it changes our picture of self, others, and world so that our life is never the same again.

This is why it can be said that we do not define such moments so much as they define us. Spirit is known by what it produces, and its fruit is always the same: *life,* and a lot more of it.

A MATTER OF LIFE AND DEATH

Spirit cannot be approached casually or practically, as if to make some compromise. It is never met halfway, but only in an all-or-nothing fashion, which is why it is met by few people and by them very seldom. On the other hand, those in rather desperate straits often meet it because they often have reasons to take risks that others would not. Whoever is at the edge, near the end, or has a lot at stake, knows personally what a life-and-death matter is and understands how inseparable the two are.

Those who are dying are among the first to look for other ways to live, and much of our being afraid to live is really a being afraid to die. So either one's living or one's dying can lead to the spirit, and spirit will always bring a person to both. Those able to die are also the ones able to live, the ones most ready to meet the spirit.

It is a gross deception to make spirit appear any less crucial than it really is. It *is* a life-and-death matter in every way that literally "drives one out of bounds," and thus we regard it with both awe and fear — the important difference between the two being that awe moves one to act while fear works to keep one from it. Whichever is uppermost will determine whether the intrusions of life pertain more to a standing in awe or an overcoming of fear — and this difference hinges on how one sees and experiences the reality of spirit.

WHAT TO LOOK FOR

What one should look for is

> . . . *moments when life unexpectedly intervenes* (a matter of spirit) . . .

Such moments stand out. We often return to them again and again in our minds. Try to recall a particular time of your own, which may have occurred suddenly in a very few minutes or have come gradually and stretched over months.

What was dying in your life then and coming to an end? And what was living or trying to begin? Where was there a little break or gap — or maybe a big one — especially in long-standing routines or habits? How did this affect your way of relating to the world? Whom did you turn to or turn away from more than before? (It seems we become friends less by what we do for one another, and more by what we live through together.) At the time did you focus more on the beginning or on what was ending? What was it that intruded, and what did you call it then? Has anything like it ever happened since, or is it, perhaps, happening now?

. . . and you rise to the occasion (a matter of soul) . . .

Such moments are times of rare *presence* when we are "all there," so that an individual touches and is touched by life in ways so new and vivid that some traces of these experiences last forever. Times so busy as these and given to such huge expenditures of energy — be they exhilarating or exasperating — are eventually exhausting too.

When context-puncture occurs, and the "more" rushes in, one feels *everything* more (more tired, more happy and sad, more scared or mad, or confused, or sure, more pleasure and more pain, and so forth) — and in a hundred ways. What specific physical effects did all this have on your own body?

. . . to take the consequences (a matter of courage) . . .

With those closest it becomes hardest. For when we no longer understand someone we know well, we usually think first that they "are not themselves." *Respect,* especially at such times as these, means giving people room to breathe and enough space to turn around in. New ways of being usually cause more than a little inconvenience and are not met with open arms, but most likely with resistance. That is why people who seek applause and desire to please others find it so difficult to grow in spirit. Strange how intensely angry human beings can get at those who choose to live. If you find this to be so, as you most likely will, it may help to remember this: anger at another's choosing to live with, is ignited mostly by anger at one's own choosing to live without.

It takes considerable courage to take the full consequences of such moments. Following context-puncture and the rush of the "more," an individual often finds a new channel or sense which can be used to move from the used to be to the yet to be. However, it is one thing to have visions on the mountain top, and another thing to lug the discovery all the way back home, there to rearrange the furniture of one's life to make room for it.

It is our not being willing to take the consequences that finally leaves us empty, lost, and not knowing what to do. If you feel this way, ask yourself:

What little bit of *new* sense was there as a seed in your moment? Did you make an attempt to actually plant it in your life and use it? Or did you keep it more as a memento to unwrap and look at now and then the way one does when opening a hope chest in the attic on a rainy afternoon?

. . . of experiencing life anew (a matter of creating) . . .

The surest sign that our special moments have staying power is that even when our picture of them changes, something remains. Because we live in the sense we make of things, which remains much the same, it is more than a little difficult for us to recognize change, especially when it is in ourselves. When the special moments of our life start to appear differently to us, however, then it is very likely that something basic in our life is beginning to change.

What has happened to the picture you have of your special moments, especially the one you selected? Do you still see it the same as you always have, or has the way you see it changed? But in working to bring your life to greater clarity, do not fall into the fatal trap of trying mostly to understand your experiences instead of *having* them; it is the latter that leads to greater understanding.

To make it easier on ourselves and others we occasionally think that only those with true "talent" (whatever that is) can be creative, and so the rest of us need not even bother to try. But ninety-five percent of creativity is *courage in action*. The many always prefer to dream of what only the few ever dare to do. So it is that we remain bound and uncreative. But spirit breaks the chains for us to courageously take the consequences of creating . . . and make a difference in life. The great reformers of the world are not trying to construct some utopia, but are simply trying to live in accordance with their souls.

Someone you do not fear at all is probably someone who cannot further you at all. And if you want and need to be stretched to experience life more, then look around until you find — and no longer need flee from — someone who out-humans you.

So, that is the matter of life and death that is well worth looking for. It should not be regarded as an assembly of various pieces, though, but as a whole that "lives and moves and has its being." To help us remember, it can all be put together as a little equation of emancipation: spirit equals soul plus courage plus creation.

SPIRITUALITY, SEXUALITY, AND THAT WHICH STIRS

The essence of spirituality is that it stirs; the essence of sexuality is that it is stirred — and it can be aroused by almost anything: a change in the weather, a piece of music, a remark or passing glance, an athletic event, a work of art, a thought or feeling . . . *anything* animal, vegetable, mineral, or spiritual.

We get it all backward and twisted around when we think our sexuality is what stirs us. We jostle, shake, and wind it, as if it were some watch that strangely stops now and then and needs a tap to get going again.

Looked at this way, the whole matter becomes a closed circle that never goes anywhere, as seen in those poor monkeys with wired hypothalamuses, who sit in labs hour after hour pressing away at the bar that artificially stimulates their pleasure center.

The mark of mature sexuality does not lie in orgasmic frequency or in the machinery running smoothly, but in being sensually open and responsive to the distinctness and immensity of what life presents us with in the world. And what opens all of that up to us is spirit.

In an acting workshop I led years back, a middle-aged woman — a librarian by profession — surprised me by wanting to do the verandah scene from Tennessee Williams's *Night of the Iguana*. She did it very well, and a few days later a verse she wrote came in the mail.

> Not making us merely
> puppets on strings,
> you help us see
> we each have wings.
>
> That irresistible force
> which you supply
> turns caterpillar
> into butterfly.

I was pleased she had gotten something out of her effort, but I felt obliged to express what might have appeared to be a minor point. I attempted to respond in kind.

That "irresistible force"
is not mine to give.
It comes to everyone
who wants to live.

Not all will see
or dare to hear it,
but the courage to be
is of the spirit.

·8·

MOVING ON TO MORE

Nowadays, to be on your way is to be home.
— *J. Pintauro*

I am done with great things and big things, great institutions and big success, and I am for those tiny invisible molecular moral forces that work from individual to individual, creeping through the crannies of the world like so many rootlets, or like the capillary oozing of water, yet which, if you give them time, will rend the hardest monuments of man's pride. — *William James*

NOTHING QUITE LIKE EXPERIENCE

By now you can see why there is no substitute for experience. For in making sense and living the sense we make, we also make our lives — our selves, our souls and bodies. Hence in our own experience we possess the means to reclaim our bodies, recover our souls, and refashion the world.

The greatest damage that can ever be done to us — other than the physical taking of our life — is not in anything others may say or do, but in our undercutting the expression of our own being in the world. We never help the being of another by wiping out our own — which is what happens when we diminish our own experiencing. Do not turn your back upon that which stirs your own experience

133

or you may lose your very soul, drifting from then on through a life about which you can never know because you no longer care. At its deepest, faith is not what many think it is; it is not a matter of living one's believing, but of believing one's living — and this is found only in and through our experiencing.

YOU KNOW YOU HAVE IT IN YOU

More than all you have done or not done, you are what you are becoming. That has in it all you have retained from what has gone before, plus the room for thoughts you haven't thought, feelings you've not yet felt, and deeds that you have never done. You may still be waiting to find out what you want to become, or you may already think you know. But knowing the *what* is not enough, you must also find your *how*, the particular way that fits and suits your soul. The right thing the wrong way, alas, is not the right thing.

And you have all that it takes to find it. Where? Right there in your own experiencing. Yet maybe this does not seem to you to amount to much of anything at all in the world. But what happens to *any* human life happens to humankind. No doubt there are splendid flowers — perhaps some of the most magnificent in all the earth — which unfold their blossoms deep in forests or jungles far away from animal trails and unseen by any eye; yet there they root, fend for themselves amidst the force and fury of life and death, participants in nature's impartial dance of no-guarantees with the environment, and finally achieve the most colorful and brilliant burst of their whole existence; living out their days warmed by sun, soaked by rain, beaten and brushed by wind and breezes, scarred by frost and insect, opened by the dawn, shut by the dark, and used by many creatures — but who would be so ignorant or so presumptuous to say of them that their life was wasted on the wilds?

You *do* have it in you. The crucial question is: Are you ready to use it fully, free yet to make your own sense and act upon it? You will not find freedom in the shallowness of "doing what you want," but in that deeper willing which enables you to pay the cost of living your way into all you want to become.

TIME FOR MOVING ON TO MORE

Ours is a time unlike any other in which to make a life. And the reason our age has no philosophy yet is because in it so many new ones are being born. It is a time when human life is changing as never before, so there is a new craving afoot, an *experience hunger* roaming the countryside in search of deeper and more substantive roots than those we have drawn sustenance from heretofore. And this hunger is there for a reason and serves a very good purpose, for *it is through re-exploring experience that we shall arrive at a re-experiencing of the world.*

This task is not for everyone and may not be for you; but if you feel in your bones that an unprecedented change has now begun, if you feel that you are a part of it or, regardless of your age, that you *want* to be, then you too are one who can sense and send the signal of our time, namely, that "it" is not full-blown at all, and is something we must experience our way into — and through. That is why, for those of us who are ready, it is time to make a start.

It is fitting that the end of this venture brings us to something that is about to begin, and the whole book can here be reduced to a single sentence for us to be on our way with: Just between us, to be somebody in a time like this, making a life in the ragged, raw real, takes seeing the soul, sensing the spirit, and moving on to more.

GLOSSARY

awareness the sense of life in the core of somebody's experience at any given moment. There are seven basic postures of human awareness.

- *thinking* is an experience of explicit meaning. It is one of the three primary realms of human experience and involves the more advanced forebrain functions of the central nervous system.
- *feeling* is an experience of implicit meaning. It is another one of the primary realms of experience and is closely involved with midbrain functions.
- *tending* is an experience of tacit meaning. It is the third primary realm of human experience and is associated with the very basic hindbrain and spinal cord functions of our central nervous system, which involve both our life-support activities (tending to) and our capacity to move on (tending toward).
- *sensing* is a mixture of feeling and tending that involves both an implicit and tacit experience of meaning.
- *intuiting* is a mixture of thinking and tending that involves an experience of both explicit and tacit meaning.
- *perceiving* is an experience-state that blends the thinking and explicit with the feeling and implicit, and it differs from judging by being oriented to gathering more information.
- *judging* is an experience-state that is a blend of thinking and feeling and the explicit and implicit, and it differs from perceiving by being oriented to obtaining greater resolution.

behesting a mode of human becoming in which one is personally involved in the historical experience of life.

beholding a mode of human becoming in which one is personally involved in the philosophical experience of life.

136

believing a mode of human becoming in which one is personally involved in the religious experience of life.

belonging a mode of human becoming in which one is personally involved in the scientific experience of life.

bespeaking a mode of human becoming in which one is personally involved in the artistic experience of life.

besteading a mode of human becoming in which one is personally involved in the political and economic experience of life.

context the set or frame of reference into which any shred of experience is put to make it meaningful.

context-puncture a break, gap, or tear in an individual's life-defining context. It occurs only in rare moments and is a time when the *more* (of one's life and the experience of it) rushes in.

dis-ease & disease — *dis-ease* is a disturbance of the soul and *disease* is a distortion of it.

embodiment the physicality of all human life and experience.

enactment the rendering of human experience into actual behavior, be it a thought, word, or deed. There is no human experience that is not embodied and enacted.

engagement an instance of two people knowingly experiencing *presence* at the same moment.

event an instance of two or more engagements occurring simultaneously and interaffecting the lives of all involved.

experience individual life in the act of *making-sense*. It is the fundament of all human life and the first indication of it. It includes *awareness* and *more*, i.e., the rest of what there is to someone outside the sense of life he or she is aware of at the moment. Experience has a primary and a secondary form; its *secondary* form is awareness, and its other form is called *primary* because awareness is contained in it and not vice versa.

insight a re-arranging of the way experience is seen by awareness. Expanding one's awareness (*secondary experience*), however, does not increase one's experience (*primary experience*). Insight often brings with it a conviction that no one else has ever made the discovery before.

making-sense the act in which life is named and known by human beings. It results in all human experience.

more & More the *more* is the rest of what is real in a person's experiencing that is outside of his or her awareness, and the *More* is the rest of what is real outside of one's experience.

motions of life the main movements that occur in varying order and in no regular sequence in the life of each individual human being. The motions of life are: experiencing, expanding, existing, exploring, excursing, exerting, exceeding, expressing, extracting, extending, and extinguishing.

soul what a human's being is becoming. It is seen in the full sweep of a life, and in that characteristic way — always as unique as one's fingerprint and developed across time — in which a person thinks, feels, tends, judges, perceives, senses, intuits, and experiences overall. All human experience affects the soul and is elaborated by it.

spirit is soul in the act of meeting and being met by the power of life anew. It is sensed in moments so special that traces of these last in a life forever. These are times when one's picture of self, others, and the world changes in such a way that one's whole life is never the same again.

stuff of human life
• human life's *background:* one's specific times, language, cultural context, and all of the other spatio-temporal "givens"

one cannot get away from.

- human life's *foreground:* the experiences through which one's life runs, from its peaks to its pits, with all of the wonderings and wanderings in between.
- human life's *belowground:* that movement or quiver at the depths of a life which manifests itself in formidable as well as fleeting ways in itches, urges, longings, and stirrings of every kind.
- human life's *aboveground:* those experiences, so hard to find the right words for, which are expressed as dreams, demons, premonitions, and other things unnamed and unknown.

wants & needs needs relate to things which an individual human being must have in order to stay alive. There are eight of these in all: food, air, water, sleep, clothing/shelter, contact/ withdrawal, elimination of waste, and experience. *Wants,* which are essentially combinations and extensions of needs, are infinite in variety and number. Unmet want produces anger, and unmet need produces pain.

LOCATOR

The Myers-Briggs Type Indicator (MBTI) is an instrument that is increasingly used to help people clarify how they prefer to approach life and deal with it as individuals. It indicates one's general orientation to experience, thus it is useful in determining fundamental strengths and in identifying more helpful behaviors one might wish to develop. It can also give a person an indication of those career-fields and work-settings one might expect to find suitable.

EXERCISE 1: Circle that letter in each of the four pairs which most fits your own experience.

The two basic ways of perceiving, or shaping what we see, are *sensing* and *intuition*. We all use both, of course, but most people begin soon in life to lean more towards one than the other.

Sensing (S) is being predominantly occupied at a given moment in touching, tasting, seeing, hearing, and smelling. The MBTI regards those for whom such acts are uppermost as S-types. On the other hand, those using *intuition* (N) spend more time looking for meanings, images, qualities, and patterns. These people are regarded as N-types.

Due to the differences in what each type focuses upon, S-types are generally more experienced at observing facts and dealing with these, while N-types are more inclined to image various possibilities and deal with those. As McCaulley and Morgan draw the difference between the two: "We might say that a sensing type is interested in seeing the individuality of each tree, while an intuitive type is more interested in the characteristics of the whole forest" (Boyles, Morgan, McCaulley, *The Health Professions,* Philadelphia: W. B. Saunders Company, 1982, p. 64).

EXPLORING THE PREFERENCES

The basic preferences distinguished in the MBTI are:

E	The extraverted attitude, in which energy and interest are directed mainly to the objects, people and events of the world	**I**	The introverted attitude, in which energy and interest are directed mainly to understanding the concepts and ideas of the world
S	Sensing perception, concerned with becoming aware of what is real, immediate and practical in experience	**N**	Intuitive perception, concerned with becoming aware of possibilities, meanings and relationships of experience
T	Thinking, which is a rational process of making decisions objectively, analytically, taking into account cause and effect	**F**	Feeling, which is a rational process of making decisions by weighing values to decide the importance of issues to oneself and to others
J	The judging attitude, in which the aim is to plan, organize and control one's environment	**P**	The perceptive attitude, in which the aim is to understand, experience, and adapt to one's environment

(The columns above are separated by "OR" between each pair.)

The eight letters stand for four mental processes (S, N, T and F) and four attitudes (E, I, J and P) which everyone uses every day. Types differ only in the fact that they prefer one of each pair, spend more time and energy in its activities, and therefore develop interests skills and motivations associated with what they have chosen.

Figure 1. The four preferences, EI, SN, TF, and JP (From McCaulley, M. H.: *Understanding the type table*. Gainesville, FL: Center for Applications of Psychological Type, 1976. This and other charts used in this section are used by permission of the authors.)

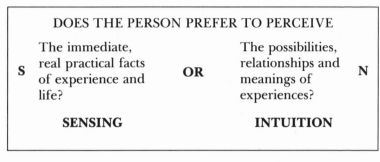

Figure 2. Sensing and intuition: two ways of becoming aware. (From McCaulley, *Understanding the type table*.)

The two ways of perceiving shape what we see, but there are two other ways we make our decisions about it. According to the MBTI, our two ways of judging are by *thinking* and *feeling*. Again, we all do both, but *thinking* tends to analyse things in a way that is somewhat detached, keeping an eye out for cause and effect and looking for logical consequences; while *feeling* — an equally rational activity — scrutinizes things in a somewhat more personal way with an eye to the values involved.

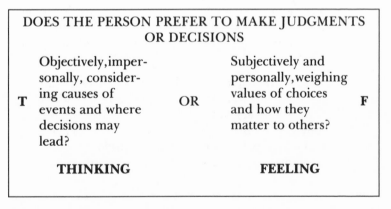

Figure 3. Thinking and feeling, two ways of making decisions. (From McCaulley, *Understanding the type table*.)

COMBINING THE PREFERENCES

Across time an individual will come to prefer one of the two ways of perceiving, and combine it with one of the two ways of judging. This then comprises that individual's basic preference-pair, which will have a persistent and pervasive influence upon his or her life. Here is a general look at the four preference-pairs as well as some of the major differences and abilities that arise out of them.

	ST	SF	NF	NT
People who prefer	SENSING + THINKING	SENSING + FEELING	INTUITION + FEELING	INTUITION + THINKING
focus their attention on	Facts	Facts	Possibilities	Possibilities
and handle these with	Impersonal analysis	Personal warmth	Personal warmth	Impersonal analysis
Thus they tend to be	Practical and matter-of-fact	Sociable and friendly	Enthusiastic and insightful	Logical and ingenious
and find scope for their abilities in	Production Construction Accounting Business Economics Law Surgery Etc.	Sales Service Customer relations Welfare work Nursing General practice Etc.	Research Teaching Preaching Counseling Writing Psychology Psychiatry Etc.	Research Science Invention Securities analysis Management Pathology Etc.

Figure 4. Some results of combinations of S, N, F, and T. (From Myers, I. B.: *Introduction to Type*. 1976. Used by permission of the author.)

Identifying one's preference-pair can be quite illuminating, but it is important to go on to determine which of the two — judging or perceiving — one prefers to engage in most, because this factor has a strong bearing upon which careers are most suitable and which settings one is likely to work in best.

DOES THE PERSON PREFER MOSTLY TO LIVE

J In a decisive, planned, and orderly way, aiming to regulate and control events?	**OR**	In a spontaneous, flexible way, aiming to understand life and adapt to it? **P**
JUDGMENT		**PERCEPTION**

Figure 5. Judging and perception, two work styles. (From McCaulley, *Understanding the type table.*)

DOES THE PERSON'S INTEREST FLOW MAINLY TO

E The outer world of actions, objects and persons?	**OR**	The inner world of concepts and ideas? **I**
EXTRAVERSION		**INTROVERSION**

Figure 6. Extraversion and introversion, two attitudes toward the world. (From McCaulley, *Understanding the type table.*)

The remaining step in identifying oneself in terms of the MBTI is to determine where one's preferences are generally the most active. Does a given individual tend to be busier in the *outer world* or in the *inner world?*

EXERCISE 2: Examine the preferences you originally circled in Exercise 1. In light of the more extended descriptions you have read, notice if there are any changes you might like to make that describe your personal preferences more accurately. If particular pairs are difficult for you to clearly determine, consider the possibility that you may be on the border between the two activities involved in that pair.

EXERCISE 3: Look at the table that follows on pages 146–49 which provides capsule descriptions of the different types found in the MBTI. This may assist you in better determining your strengths and mode of effectiveness by seeing it in relation to those of others.

Sensing Types

With Thinking	*With Feeling*
ISTJ	**ISFJ**
Serious, quiet, earn success by concentration and thoroughness. Practical, orderly, matter-of-fact, logical, realistic and dependable. See to it that everything is well organized. Take responsibility. Make up their own minds as to what should be accomplished and work toward it steadily, regardless of protests or distractions.	Quiet, friendly, responsible and conscientious. Work devotedly to meet their obligations and serve their friends and school. Thorough, painstaking, accurate. May need time to master technical subjects, as their interests are not often technical. Patient with detail and routine. Loyal, considerate, concerned with how other people feel.
Live their outer life more with thinking, inner more with sensing.	Live their outer life more with feeling, inner more with sensing.
ISTP	**ISFP**
Cool onlookers, quiet, reserved, observing and analyzing life with detached curiosity and unexpected flashes of original humor. Usually interested in impersonal principles, cause and effect, or how and why mechanical things work. Exert themselves no more than they think necessary, because any waste of energy would be inefficient.	Retiring, quietly friendly, sensitive, modest about their abilities. Shun disagreements, do not force their opinions or values on others. Usually do not care to lead but are often loyal followers. May be rather relaxed about assignments or getting things done, because they enjoy the present moment and do not want to spoil it by undue haste or exertion.
Live their outer life more with sensing, inner more with thinking.	Live their outer life more with sensing, inner more with feeling.

Judging and *Perceptive* label the rows; *Introverts* labels the group.

Figure 7. Effects of the combinations of the four preferences on young people. (From Myers, I. B.: *Introduction to Type.*)

Sensing Types

With Thinking	*With Feeling*	
ESTP	**ESFP**	
Matter-of-fact, do not worry or hurry, enjoy whatever comes along. Tend to like mechanical things and sports, with friends on the side. May be a bit blunt or insensitive. Can do math or science when they see the need. Dislike long explanations. Are best with real things that can be worked, handled, taken apart or put back together. Live their outer life more with sensing, inner more with thinking.	Outgoing, easygoing, accepting, friendly, fond of a good time. Like sports and making things. Know what's going on and join in eagerly. Find remembering facts easier than mastering theories. Are best in situations that need sound common sense and practical ability with people as well as with things. Live their outer life more with sensing, inner more with feeling.	Perceptive
ESTJ	**ESFJ**	
Practical realists, matter-of-fact, with a natural head for business or mechanics. Not interested in subjects they see no use for, but can apply themselves when necessary. Like to organize and run activities. Tend to run things well, especially if they remember to consider other people's feelings and points of view when making their decisions. Live their outer life more with thinking, inner more with sensing.	Warm-hearted, talkative, popular, conscientious, born cooperators, active committee members. Always doing something nice for someone. Work best with plenty of encouragement and praise. Little interest in abstract thinking or technical subjects. Main interest is in things that directly and visibly affect people's lives. Live their outer life more with feeling, inner more with sensing.	Judging

Extraverts

Intuitives

With Feeling	*With Thinking*
INFJ	**INTJ**
Succeed by perseverance, originality and desire to do whatever is needed or wanted. Put their best efforts into their work. Quietly forceful, conscientious, concerned for others. Respected for their firm principles. Likely to be honored and followed for their clear convictions as to how best to serve the common good.	Have original minds and great drive which they use only for their own purposes. In fields that appeal to them they have a fine power to organize a job and carry it through with or without help. Skeptical, critical, independent, determined, often stubborn. Must learn to yield less important points in order to win the most important.
Live their outer life more with feeling, inner more with intuition.	Live their outer life more with thinking, inner more with intuition.
INFP	**INTP**
Full of enthusiasms and loyalties, but seldom talk of these until they know you well. Care about learning, ideas, language, and independent projects of their own. Apt to be on yearbook staff, perhaps as editor. Tend to undertake too much, then somehow get it done. Friendly, but often too absorbed in what they are doing to be sociable or notice much.	Quiet, reserved, brilliant in exams, especially in theoretical or scientific subjects. Logical to the point of hair-splitting. Interested mainly in ideas, with little liking for parties or small talk. Tend to have very sharply defined interests. Need to choose careers where some strong interest of theirs can be used and useful.
Live their outer life more with intuition, inner more with feeling.	Live their outer life more with intuition, inner more with thinking.

Left margin labels: Judging, Perceptive (under Introverts)

Intuitives

With Feeling	*With Thinking*	
ENFP	**ENTP**	Perceptive
Warmly enthusiastic, high-spirited, ingenious, imaginative. Able to do almost anything that interests them. Quick with a solution for any difficulty and ready to help anyone with a problem. Often rely on their ability to improvise instead of preparing in advance. Can always find compelling reasons for whatever they want. Live their outer life more with intuition, inner more with feeling.	Quick, ingenious, good at many things. Stimulating company, alert and outspoken, argue for fun on either side of a question. Resourceful in solving new and challenging problems, but may neglect routine assignments. Turn to one new interest after another. Can always find logical reasons for whatever they want. Live their outer life more with intuition, inner more with thinking.	
ENFJ	**ENTJ**	Judging
Responsive and responsible. Feel real concern for what others think and want, and try to handle things with due regard for other people's feelings. Can present a proposal or lead a group discussion with ease and tact. Sociable, popular, active in school affairs, but put time enough on their studies to do good work. Live their outer life more with feeling, inner more with intuition.	Hearty, frank, able in studies, leaders in activities. Usually good in anything that requires reasoning and intelligent talk, such as public speaking. Are well-informed and keep adding to their fund of knowledge. May sometimes be more positive and confident than their experience in an area warrants. Live their outer life more with thinking, inner more with intuition.	

Extraverts

"IF YOU PIONEER, PIONEER ON PURPOSE"*

We believe all careers can benefit from the talents of all 16 types. All types may be found in all fields. So far, no research proves that any type will always be unhappy and incompetent in any career — and we doubt that such a research finding will ever occur. We do know, however, that all types are not equally attracted to careers or to all the specialties within a career. If you are thinking of a field that has attracted relatively few of your type, consider how much you like to pioneer and be different. Some people enjoy pioneering, and others are uncomfortable in settings where other people look at life differently from the way they do. This is why we recommend that if you enter a field where your type is less represented, do it consciously and with your eyes open. Then the differences can be used as interesting, challenging, and sometimes amusing events that help you learn instead of getting in your way.

In whatever way you have used the information, you should have learned some useful ways of thinking about yourself and about careers. You have learned two important facts: Each field is more attractive to some types than to others, and there is room for every type in every occupation. This means you can use the information to guide your thinking, but you should not conclude that any field is not for you simply because others of your type seldom enter it.

---

*Reprinted with permission from Mary McCaulley and Margaret Morgan, "The Health Professions: Characteristics and Student Self-Assessment," in Boyles et al., *The Health Professions* (Philadelphia: W. B. Saunders Co., 1982), pp. 54–78.

NOTE: Those interested in actually taking the MBTI can contact a licensed psychologist in their own community.

FOR THOSE WHO WANT TO READ MORE

There is always another book to be read — especially the newest one. In reading, one thing leads to another, so just by sticking to the main road one will come across those good books which are referred to and cited most often. The good ones that are off the beaten path are the ones harder to come by, so a few are mentioned here that throw broad beams of light on important aspects of human experience.

Written in 1874, *Psychology from an Empirical Standpoint* (Humanities Press, New York, 1973) is the classic work of the priest, philosopher and psychologist Franz Brentano, of whom many have never heard, though he was truly a pivotal figure in history in that (a) his were the only nonmedical lectures a then-obscure student named Sigmund Freud attended regularly, (b) he had an overwhelming influence on Husserl and used the term "phenomenology" prior to him, and (c) his work was so suggestive that it gave a truly formative impetus to such a variety of movements as the Language Analysis (*Sprachkritik*) of the Vienna Circle, Heidegger and Existentialism, subsequent developments in the psychology of Self, and Gestalt psychology.

Ironically, it was when "soul" was losing most of what it had meant in western civilization for well over two thousand years, that the so-called "science of the soul," modern psychology, was founded. And it was at that time that Brentano forged a foundation for it which anticipated the course it would mainly take for the next hundred years — all of which is carefully recounted in the late Antos C. Rancurello's *A Study Of Franz Brentano* (Academic Press, New York, 1968), which contains a complete bibliography on Brentano's books and on the scholarly work about him. Reading Brentano can enable one to pick up again on strands which many have long since lost hold of, e.g., the role of theory and method in science and thought, and the importance of *act* in all psychology — not to mention his lifelong labors, sparked by his esteemed teacher Aristotle, to bring as much clarity as possible to the meaning of "soul."

Horace Freeland Judson's *Eighth Day of Creation* (Simon & Schuster, New York, 1979) recounts in fascinating detail the step-by-step discoveries which ultimately led to the unraveling of the molecular structure of DNA by Crick and Watson in 1953, ushering in a revolution in biology comparable to that begun in physics when Einstein came forth with the theory of relativity in 1905.

Karl Pribram and Merton Gill show in *Freud's 'Project' Reassessed* (Harper & Row, New York, 1978) the importance of the often forgotten fact that Freud was a physiologist who, unlike so very many of his followers, endeavored to plant his theories in the firm ground of the biological functioning of the human organism — so much so, in fact, that this usually overlooked work of his can, as the authors demonstrate, serve as a sort of primer, a fine "Preface to Contemporary Cognitive Theory and Neuropsychology."

One of the few alive today who is able to make philosophy both readable and worthwhile is Princeton's Walter Kaufmann, whose *Discovering the Mind* (McGraw-Hill, New York, 1980) attempts to get philosophy back on a more productive track by taking a critical look at the past two centuries of our intellectual history in the West to see where things went awry. His definition of "mind" in this recent three-volume series is worth observing here: "And when I speak of the mind I am not contrasting it with heart or soul, as do those who associate the mind with the intellect and the heart or soul with emotion. I use "mind" as an inclusive term for feeling and intelligence, reason and emotion, perception and will, thought and the unconscious." Because his natural style is quite polemical (especially in books like his excellent *Critique of Religion and Philosophy*), it unfortunately keeps some people from seeing the genuine worth of his provocative thinking as well as the rare richness of a mind able to combine the philosophic and artistic with elements of the scientific and religious.

Confucius to Cummings (New Directions, New York, 1964), edited by Ezra Pound and Marcella Spaan, may be one of only a half dozen poetry anthologies ever compiled that are not seeped in the pedantic. Pound's ever-prickly genius stands out in his peppery comments, which are interspersed throughout this valuable book, and Spaan's concise contributions are illuminating. *Do not skip the appendixes at the back for "Instructors,"* which has much to say in such a refreshing vein as this, for example: "Don't fall for the dodge that there are 5,000 things you need to know; such ideas are spread abroad by those who don't know anything well but may have invested a lot of time getting an "education." One or two books will put you way ahead of almost everyone, if they are important books and you *know* them. The possibility of a Renaissance may depend upon the number who grasp this fact." To me, the poem "The Soul and the Body" by John Davies (1569–1626) is magnificent and worth the cost of the entire volume itself.

World Population and Human Values: A New Reality (Harper & Row, New York, 1981) by Jonas and Jonathan Salk is an easier-on-the-eye expanded version of Jonas Salk's central thesis laid out in *The Survival of the Wisest* and alluded to earlier in Chapter 2. *Mind and Nature: A Necessary Unity* (E.P. Dutton, New York, 1979) reflects the creative genius of the late Gregory Bateson, whose work urges us to try to see biological evolution as a *mental* process, which is the way he himself came to view it as the result of a lifetime of scientific work and reflection. And those with little prior acquaintance of studies on the human body might begin with *Principles of Anatomy and Physiology* by Gerard Tortora and Nicholas Anagnostakos (Harper & Row, New York, 1975). Some books are slicker or shorter, but few if any are sounder than this well-written, clearly organized, and amply illustrated text that starts with atoms, moves on to explain chemical bonds, and then works up to the fully functioning body of the human adult — covering in sufficient yet interesting detail each of the body's eleven major systems. Helpful questions are given in each section to break the content down into digestible portions.

The Therapy of the Word in Classical Antiquity (Yale University Press, New Haven, 1970) is a most intriguing scholarly exploration into the way classical philosophers, principally Plato and Aristotle, saw and dealt with the power that the *word* has to act as a force on a person or soul — a principle wittingly or unwittingly made use of in all therapy, but which, unfortunately, "the Greek physicians were not wise enough to take up and make their own." Those interested in making their way further into personality theory will find one of genuine originality and considerable integrity in George A. Kelly's *A Theory of Personality*, which is a contribution to "the psychology of personal constructs" and contains his fundamental assertion that "A person's processes are psychologically channelized by the ways in which he anticipates events" (W.W. Norton, New York, 1963).

The Art Spirit (J.B. Lippincott Company, New York, 1960) is the compilation of the painter Robert Henri's classes on art. It was printed in the 1920s and is written in a style that makes it seem one is sitting in a group of students in his studio; you can hear and almost see him speaking as he relates painting to his conception of art, and shows how it is a way of life. Heinrich Wolfflin's classic *The Sense of Form in Art* (Chelsea Publishing, New York, 1958) is a compare-and-contrast approach to German and Italian Renaissance art, showing how cultural differences — like those of northern and southern Europe — can have striking effects on how painters taught by the same masters and, sometimes, even painting the same scenes, construe it in vividly different ways. Also in the area of art, Ortega's *Phenomenology And Art* (W.W. Norton, New York, 1975) is a splendid collection of a number of his essays dealing with phenomenological issues in philosophy and art, many of which are central to the whole question of how human beings perceive and experience reality.

Those who wish to investigate "soul" in its religious context, in addition to its philosophical one, should see Johs. Pedersen's outstanding two-volume *Israel: Its Life and Culture* (Oxford University Press, London, 1959), especially the section in the first volume entitled "The Soul, Its Powers and Capacity." And Helmut Thielicke's *A Little Exercise for Young Theologians* (Ferdmans Publishing, Grand Rapids, 1962) packs so much wisdom into its forty pages that it is difficult to describe. Written in the creative hiatus of a sabbatical leave — which explains a lot — it contains such soul-searching gems as, "Even an orthodox theologian can be spiritually dead, while perhaps a heretic crawls on forbidden bypaths to the sources of life."

In a class by itself is *Cell & Psyche: The Biology of Purpose* (Harper & Brothers, New York, 1961) by Edmund Sinnott, who presents in this little monograph a most profound picture of how the biological and psychological aspects of human life are organismically interrelated.

Any *one* of these books, when read and thoroughly digested, will open an individual to more of life and thus make possible a greater experience of it.

Now, as a fitting end to all bookish ventures — including the one between these covers — there is this little verse by Johann Scheffler, who wrote under the name of "Angelus Silesius" when he penned in German over three hundred years ago:

> Freund, es ist genug. Im
> Fall du mehr willst lesen,
> So geh und werde selbst die
> Schrift und selbst das Wesen.

Which, when translated freely with a sense of its rhyme, goes like this:

> Friend, it is enough.
> If you still want to read some,
> Then go 'till you yourself become,
> Both the writing and the stuff.